DISCARD

✓   JAN 9 4

ALSO BY IRENE DARIA

The Fashion Cycle

Lutèce

★ ★ ★ ★

Lutèce

A DAY IN THE LIFE OF AMERICA'S GREATEST RESTAURANT

★ ★ ★ ★

IRENE DARIA

RANDOM HOUSE
NEW YORK

Library of Congress Cataloging-in-Publication Data
Daria, Irene.
Lutèce : a day in the life of America's greatest restaurant /
Irene Daria. — 1st ed.
p.   cm.
ISBN 0-394-58964-5
1. Lutèce (Restaurant)   2. Restaurants—New York (N.Y.)
I. Title.
TX945.5.L88D37   1993
641.5′09747′1—dc20   93-20429

Manufactured in the United States of America
2 4 6 8 9 7 5 3
First Edition

Book design by Oksana Kushnir

This book is dedicated to Cary R. Wiener,
the best husband, friend, lawyer,
reader, and adviser in the whole wide world.

ACKNOWLEDGMENTS

Special thanks to Eric Ashworth, to David Rosenthal and
Ruth Fecych at Random House, and to André Soltner
and the staff of Lutèce, who good-naturedly put up with
being observed and questioned for an entire year.

INTRODUCTION

There are certain laws that govern the universe: every morning the sun rises; every year you have a birthday; every Friday, if you live in New York and like to go out to eat or are a part of the food world, you reach for the weekend section of *The New York Times*. This section of the paper carries the restaurant-review column, and the number of stars this column awards a restaurant can be a matter of life and death.

For New York City's Lutèce, a modest twenty-nine-table establishment, and its equally modest owner and chef, André Soltner, the review has always been cause for celebration. Of the more than ten thousand restaurants in New York City, on the average fewer than six have four-star status at any one time. Lutèce is one of them and has been for decades. Almost uniquely, it has been awarded four stars by three different *New York Times* reviewers.

Of course, there are other New York City newspapers and magazines, and for people who visit New York but don't keep up with the local press, there are restaurant reviews published in book form, the most influential and the most publicized of which is the *Mobil Travel Guide.*

Approximately eight thousand restaurants across the country were reviewed for the 1993 edition of this guide, and only twelve of them received five stars, the guide's top ranking. Lutèce was one of them. In fact, Lutèce has received five stars from the *Mobil Travel Guide* for twenty-two consecutive years, bested only by The Maisonette in Ohio, a five-star winner for twenty-nine consecutive years, and Ernie's in San Francisco, which has been awarded five stars in thirty nonconsecutive years.

Obviously, all of these glowing reviews have been quite good for Lutèce's business. We Americans are a nation of followers. We like reviews. We read them. We *listen* to them. Ask yourself: If money was not an issue, where would you take a client you had to impress? Where would you celebrate a special occasion? In a restaurant that had received a top-ranking five or four stars or in one that had received three, two, or one? I'd pick a top-rated restaurant. That's why, when it came to selecting one restaurant to showcase the behind-the-scenes workings of the restaurant world, I chose to write about Lutèce. I am a journalist, not a food critic, and I stress that my goal was not to validate or disprove Lutèce's high ranking but to show the work involved in maintaining it.

This unpretentious restaurant began its rise to culinary fame twenty years ago, when André Soltner became its sole owner in 1973. It has been at the pinnacle of the American food world for almost as long. Unsurprisingly, its name has become a metaphor for excellence. Even hot-dog vendors who have never set foot in the establishment have been overheard muttering to dissatisfied customers: "What do you think this is? Lutèce?"

So great is this restaurant's reputation and so steady its following that at first it seemed it would be unaffected by the downturn in the American economy. The business was untouched by the 1987 stock market crash, and as recently as 1989, if you didn't make reservations one month ahead, you were out of luck. Aspiring diners began calling at nine in the morning, and by nine-thirty the place was booked for the same date the following month. Hundreds were turned away.

But then came the recession of 1990–91. Many of the business people who make up the bulk of Lutèce's clientele lost their jobs or had their expense accounts severely curtailed. All across the city trendy restaurants began folding, and a few high-end places like Metro, Prunelle, Hubert's, and Le Cygne closed their doors forever. Old-line establishments such as the "21" Club and The Four Seasons dropped some of their prices or created special lower-cost price-fixed dinners.

This time a cold wind blew through Lutèce. Empty tables began to appear in its dining rooms. By the fall of 1991 business had fallen by 15 percent, although annual sales still hovered above an impressive $4 million.

Even so, captains and waiters were being told not to show up for some meals because there wasn't enough work to keep them busy, and the day bartender began whispering to the coat-check woman, "You know how many people were here for dinner last night?" and revealing an ominously low number. Suddenly staff members, normally too busy to say more than a passing word to each other, were reminiscing about the good old days, when even in the middle of terrible snowstorms that left most restaurants begging for business, Lutèce would still pack them in.

Everywhere—in the kitchen, in the dining room, at the bar—employees were furrowing their brows over the slow business. Even André Soltner, Lutèce's chef and owner, prepared himself for a previously unimaginable possibility. "If it grows worse," he said, his English laced with an Alsatian accent, "if we are ever off twenty or thirty percent, then we'll have to think about layoffs."

There was nothing André could do but wait and try to do business as usual. Then, food writing being the illogical, subjective thing that it is, at the peak of the empty-table epidemic, on May 15,

1991, *The New York Times* printed a story headlined, "Reserving a Table: Less Waiting, Except at Lutèce and Bouley."

It was an odd headline, since the reporter noted that she had been able to get a same-day reservation at Lutèce for 6:00 P.M., and she quoted André Soltner as saying that the restaurant did not fill up "all the time for lunch." Other restaurants were said to be equally busy. Nonetheless the headline writer singled out Lutèce and Bouley (the youngest of New York's four-star restaurants) as places where reservations were hard to get.

Even though it was incorrect, the headline reaffirmed the general public's impression of Lutèce. It was the leader of the pack. It was still the place to go. Among long-established restaurants, it was still the hardest to get into. And so people once again tried to get in.

How did this headline happen to get written? Was the headline writer blinded by Lutèce's reputation? Or did the writer simply wish it was true? Although some people grumble that they just don't see what's so special about Lutèce, many more love it. They want it to survive. They want it to *thrive*. They want André to continue getting the adoration he has become used to and on which his personal satisfaction depends.

Scan the hundreds of articles and reviews that have been written on the place and you are sure to be nauseated by the cloying, worshipful tones. I read much of this press coverage in one sitting, before I had eaten at Lutèce or met André, and my response was, "Oh, come on. Give me a break. What's everybody drooling about?" This book will answer that question. It will also show you what a restaurant must do to get a top ranking of four or five stars. It needs to use the best and freshest ingredients and to prepare them in a tasteful, consistent manner, in which the flavors complement rather than overwhelm each other. It must have an excellent service staff, and it needs to have an owner on the premises, attending to all the little details and making the customers feel special and welcome. Simply put, in order to get four or five stars, a restaurant needs to perfectly execute its own individual goals.

Sometimes those goals and the goals the restaurant's customers wish it had set for itself are different. Take my friend Donna, for example. She recently visited Lutèce for the first time, and although she said the service was excellent, she didn't like the food. "It was heavy," she said by way of criticism.

What would a professional restaurant critic say to that? "Donna is a middle-of-the-road diner," said Thomas Kelly, director of inspections for the American Express Distinguished Restaurants of North America Award Program and a restaurant professor at Cornell University's School of Hotel and Restaurant Management. "Her knowledge of cuisine on a worldwide scale is limited. Her comment about it being heavy was said in a negative tone. But criticizing André Soltner's Lutèce for being heavy is like criticizing an Indian restaurant for serving curry. If you don't drink Scotch, you shouldn't comment on the vagaries of single-malt Scotches, because you don't like it in the first place—and that's what she did."

A wholesale vegetable purveyor I interviewed doesn't think much of Lutèce either and claims that the food at the Park Ridge Diner in Park Ridge, New Jersey, is equal to or better than the food at Lutèce.

"I will take you to the Park Ridge Diner or the Eldorado diner [in the Bronx] and you will have a piece of salmon [such as] you have not in your life had before," he told me. "With this salmon, which is enough to choke a horse, you will get two vegetables, bread, a very, very fine salad with a very, very nice dressing of your choice and a beverage, all for twelve dollars and ninety-five cents.

"Soltner will give you his younger brother, which will weigh about a half an ounce, and glop it up with all kinds of sauces, and he will make nice, beautiful vegetables in animal shapes or whatever and a sprig of something, and he'll present that to you in his toque and you will pay forty dollars [actually thirty-eight dollars for lunch] or sixty-five dollars [sixty dollars for dinner]. You will leave hungry and you will say, 'Gee, it was great.' "

The purveyor grants that at Lutèce the ambience is a little better than at the diner, "but speaking only about the food . . . Lutèce will buy asparagus and so will the Eldorado diner. It's the same asparagus, no different. The tomatoes are the same tomatoes."

True? No, and I'll address that point later. But true or not, my friend Donna and the vegetable wholesaler are entitled to their opinions. So was the late Malcolm Forbes, who left André a bequest of one thousand dollars in his will, "as a token of gratitude for the joy your skills and genius added to the lives of those who have been lucky and sensible enough to dine at your restaurant." Obviously, Forbes liked Lutèce, and since he owned *Forbes* magazine, the publication frequently gave Lutèce glowing reviews.

The views shared by Donna and the vegetable purveyor will never be published in a restaurant-review column. This is because publishers now generally demand that aspiring professional restaurant critics must be trained cooks or at least have worked in the industry. It's important for us to remember, however, that even food critics with culinary training should never have the last word, and that they disagree even among themselves.

Perhaps no one evoked more disagreement than Jane Freiman, who, in her November 8, 1991, review of Lutèce in *New York Newsday,* gave the restaurant a devastating two and a half stars. She criticized the preparation of some of the food and said it was too old-fashioned. She delivered a crushing blow to André, even though, he says, "Someone told me she asked them the difference between a mousse of duckling and foie gras. Here's someone who judges me and doesn't know the difference between foie gras and mousse. So [what she says] doesn't bother me, but the people who read it don't know that. Who is she to give me stars? She is not knowledgeable enough in cuisine to judge me, to give me stars. That bothers me. The system bothers me."

"I know what question he's referring to, and his understanding of it is inaccurate," counters Freiman. "I asked that question in confidence of one of his suppliers. I wasn't asking the difference between foie gras and mousse, which is something I know perfectly well. I had a question about the texture and flavor of a terrine of foie gras I ate at Lutèce, and it's not to André's credit that I had that question. To me, what I ate tasted like a preprepared product, and it would be inexcusable for a restaurant of Lutèce's caliber to serve a preprepared product. Before I said that what I ate wasn't pure foie gras I had to verify its identity. Restaurant critics have been sued for saying that French fries were frozen or that there was cheese in something when there wasn't.

"So I called the supplier and asked whether André purchased whole foie gras or a mousse. I was told André didn't buy any mousse, that he bought only the best quality foie gras, and that he took it and made his own terrine with it. In retrospect, the taste was probably affected by the seasonings used and the age of the product.

"Every time I criticize a French restaurant they get very offended and they look for a way to dismiss that criticism," Freiman continues. "André's way of doing that was by questioning my qualifications. He wouldn't have said what he said if I were a man or if I were married to someone who was French. I lived in France, I was a French major in college, I studied cooking in France, I did a *stage* [guest visitation] in a number of French kitchens, and I've taught French cooking. My qualifications are not the issue and I stand by what I said in the review.

"This was not an easy review for me to write," Freiman goes on. "I went seven or eight times to Lutèce, which is much more than I would normally go. I was bending over backward to be fair. The first five times I didn't get recognized, and then I did and the service I got when I was recognized was better than when I wasn't. My review was nothing personal. It wasn't an indictment of him. He's a charming man, and this year I nominated him for the 1993 James Beard award for lifetime achievement in gastronomy. He's done more for French cooking in this country than perhaps any other chef. I didn't enjoy writing that review. It was a tough thing to do. But I stand by what I wrote. He can't dismiss it."

Far from dismissing it, André began doubting himself. "Did I reach a stage where, without knowing it, I don't make it in the right way anymore?" he asked himself. "Am I not anymore on the right track?"

André would look to *The New York Times* for the answer. He

knew that the all-powerful, perhaps *too* powerful, *New York Times* had a review in the works. Bryan Miller, the *Times*'s restaurant reviewer, had been at the restaurant a lot recently, and a *Times* fact checker had called to check the restaurant's prices and hours. That meant the review could appear on any upcoming Friday.

André worried about that review. "What if the *Times* gives us three stars, two, or even one?" he thought. If that happened, he says, he would ask himself, "Should I continue or should I not continue? Being in this business for forty-three years, Lutèce thirty-one years, I think this question would [arise] in my mind. And even maybe would be a reason to give up, to throw in the sponge.

"What reason do I have to continue? If I work five more years or ten more, or if I stop today, it would not be a big difference. The only reason to continue is if we are encouraged to do it. But if on the contrary we are hammered down, with reason, maybe, that would tell you, 'Okay. That's it.' "

While André waits for his review, let us sit in on a day at Lutèce in November 1991. Although this day is a composite, all the events described took place during the year I was an observer at the restaurant. And though this book is centered on Lutèce, it serves as a window to the world of all restaurants, covering food preparation, suppliers, customers, food critics, laws, inspections, the seemingly endless hours of work. I hope that reading it will make your experience of restaurants a more enlightened one, because, no matter which restaurant you go to, as you clink glasses with your dining companions, you will know what is going on behind the closed kitchen door across the room. You will be aware of the complicated logistics involved in putting the food on your plate. You will also have some understanding of what makes a great chef run . . . the fear of failure.

"You see, if tomorrow I don't deliver or if tomorrow I don't cook good, or if tomorrow people think I don't cook well, then everything is kaput," André says. "If I give up a little bit, in three months people will say, 'Oh, André is no good anymore. André doesn't take care of his restaurant. It's not what it used to be. Blah, blah, blah.' So I have to stay very much on top of things. Just because you satisfied somebody ten times, you can't let it go for the next two times. Maybe one time they will forgive you and say, 'Well, maybe he had a bad day.' They don't forgive you a second time. That I know. That I'm sure. The customers don't owe me anything." The fear that one day his customers or the reviewers may decide he is not good anymore is "in my conscious mind all the time."

Lutèce

★ ★ ★ ★

$\mathcal{T}$ARTE À L'OIGNON

FOR 6 PEOPLE

Crust:

2 cups flour
¹/₂ cup sweet butter

1 tsp salt
¹/₂ cup cold water

Onion mixture:

1 lb. onions
2 Tb sweet butter
1 egg

¹/₂ cup heavy cream
Salt, pepper, nutmeg

Preheat oven to 375 degrees.

Prepare crust. With a pastry blender or two knives cut the butter into the flour. Add salt and water. Mix with hands until just combined. Wrap in waxed paper and refrigerate for 30 minutes.

Chop onions and cook them gently in the butter. They should be slightly browned.

Beat eggs and cream together. Add to the onions. Stir in salt, pepper, and nutmeg.

Put crust in 10-inch pie tin. Fill with the onion mixture.

Bake at 375 degrees for 25 minutes.

Serve very hot.

NOTE: One of Lutèce's most beloved dishes.

5:30 A.M.

Having gone to bed at two in the morning, André Soltner and his wife, Simone, are sleeping on the fourth floor of 249 East Fiftieth Street, where both their home and their restaurant are situated. Their sleep is the sound rest of those who have succeeded in their lives' missions. He has dedicated his life to cooking, a career that has earned him accolades, financial security, and fame. Hers is a quieter success, the nurturing of a loving marriage that began in 1962, the year after Lutèce opened.

It would be easy to romanticize their lives—he creating stellar meals to be eaten by former presidents and first ladies, movie stars and celebrity fashion designers, as well as by less well known but equally welcome clients, she standing just inside the front door, greeting and seating the guests.

It would be easy to envy them, but André won't let you. "Our life is not beautiful," he says. "I love it but sometimes I feel sorry for my wife. We've been married more than thirty years and I didn't give her too much. We never go to the movies, the theater. Our lives are not examples of full lives."

When *Time* magazine asked Simone what she would do if André ever did the unimaginable and sold Lutèce, Simone replied, "I would live."

Feel the weight of those words and what they say about the restaurant business. In any other field, when you get to the top you can slack off a little bit, you can take on fewer projects, cases, patients, singing engagements. In a restaurant you play to a full house twice a day, whether you feel like it or not. This is the equivalent of holding a meeting with ninety of your clients at the same time. Everyone wants your attention. They all think you are there only for them. And everyone's a critic. Anyone who's ever wielded a whisk believes he or she can do better than you. People think what you do is easy—cook meals and charge three, four, or five times what they cost you to prepare, and charge two and a half times the average retail cost of a bottle of wine that you bought wholesale. What a way to make an easy fortune.

What a way to lose your shirt. Sixty percent of the new restaurants that open nationwide close or change hands within the first five years, according to the New York Restaurant Association, which lobbies Albany on behalf of six thousand food service establishments throughout the state and tracks statistical data on the industry. In New York the statistics on restaurant closings are even more striking: 75 percent of new restaurants close or are sold within five years. And that's during a strong economy.

Why has Lutèce survived at the top for so long? Perfectly executed food is only half the answer. The other half lies in the fact that André Soltner makes his customers feel welcome, well cared for, and, at the risk of making cynics scoff, loved. In fact, André considers a love of people to be one of the defining characteristics of a great chef: "Cooking for someone is like having a love affair," he says. "You cook to make someone happy. A great chef, he has to have great talent for cooking, but if he has only great talent for cooking, it's not enough. The end of the cooking is to cook the best you can to give somebody pleasure. That's the whole thing of cooking—the better it is, the more pleasure you have. I'm sure somebody with a bitter character cannot be a good chef. Because he's bitter he doesn't love the people. To make someone feel good you have to love the person. Not love like husband and wife but still love. If you don't have that you cannot cook.

"We have quite a few chefs here and in Europe that get spoiled by their . . ." He puffs out his cheeks. "I think we are guys who should remember where our place is, you know. We are guys who are here to cook, we are here to sell soups. But lately, in the last ten or fifteen years, we got so much publicity that we are in the limelight and many of my colleagues cannot handle it. They don't stay modest enough, and that takes away from their approach with other people, from making people feel comfortable in the restaurant. Our customers don't come to get a lesson. They come to enjoy themselves."

And to eat the food. But André is the first to admit that he and his staff suffer from off days. "People are very demanding," he says. "They expect from us that it is always perfect. It should be but it cannot be all the time like that. We have our failures too. People expect from us all the time the top, and that's what they are paying for, but who in the world is always perfect? We try, but I know that we are not always the best. But people don't want to know that.

"Most of the time we cook out of love, and that is the best way," he continues, "but there are days when you don't feel like cooking but you still know the techniques because you are a professional. Those are our off days, when we cook just by technique. If a painter doesn't feel like painting he doesn't have to. I have to deliver if I feel like it or not."

When he doesn't feel like it, it's usually for good reason, since the problems he, and all restaurateurs, deal with are endless and would cramp anyone's inspiration. These problems arise even though the restaurant business is characterized by repetition—many of the tasks André and his staff perform, they do day in and day out. The same vegetables have to be peeled, the same sauces prepared, the same tables set, the same dining rooms cleaned. The surprise element comes from all the things that can and do go wrong. This happens so often that André says, "I worry for this country. No one cares about doing their jobs right."

The scenarios are endless: His supplier delivers the wrong order, or the merchandise is not fresh. His oven or mixer breaks down and the repairman doesn't show up. The linen company forgets to pick up his laundry and he runs short of clean linen. The wine or liquor supplier raises his prices and hopes André won't notice. The glass supplier delivers wrong-size glasses and now the restaurant's glasses are mismatched. Or maybe one of his customers says or does something upsetting, an event that happens rather frequently.

"Some customers are very hard to please," says André. "They come here to see what we do wrong. Chefs are very sensitive people. It's happened at times that I've recommended specials to customers and they've said to me, 'What? Are you trying to get rid of this?'

"That makes something inside me . . ." He pushes an imaginary knife into his chest and twists it. "I stop right there and say, 'Well, then, you can take a look at the menu and the captain will be right over to take your order.' I never talk to them again."

Or, he says, "People get very upset when their tables are not ready at the exact time that they are supposed to be. I know that a restaurant of our price range and caliber should have the table ready. I know that. But sometimes you can't control it. The table who sat down at six and told you they would be done by eight may be running ten minutes late and that affects your seating plans for the rest of the night. But people don't realize that.

"One night a man came in wearing a tuxedo with a party of eight. He had a reservation for eight o'clock. My wife said, 'I'm sorry but could you please wait five minutes?' and he said to her, 'I am the chairman of the board of a bank and you expect me to wait for a table?'

"The way my wife reacts, her defense, is that she stops talking. She becomes totally silent. Me, I am a little smoother. I saw the whole thing and went out with a big smile and said, 'Hello. I am the owner. I am very sorry you will have to wait five minutes for your table, but if you wait I will do everything I can to ensure you have a very enjoyable evening here at Lutèce.'

"He said, 'I am the chairman of the board of a bank and you expect me to wait five minutes for a table?'

"I said, 'I am the chairman of the board of Lutèce, and if I went to a bank I would have to wait for more than five minutes. You can either do the same or you can leave.' They left."

During one of the many mornings I spent with André, among the numerous phone calls he received was one from a woman who was irate because when she had called the day before to reserve a table in the downstairs dining room, Simone had told her she could not guarantee it. The woman kept insisting that she wanted that table and Simone insisted right back that it could not be promised.

After André got on the phone the woman talked and talked, saying she had been treated rudely, until finally André said, "Excuse me, but I was nearby and I heard what happened. You were insisting that you need a table at nine o'clock downstairs and—" The woman cut him off and André listened until he interrupted, saying, "I'm very sorry about that but I was a little closer and what happened is—" Again the woman wouldn't let him finish his sentence. He listened and then, referring to his wife, said, "And the lady, she—" Again he got cut off. "That's fine," he ultimately said. "At nine o'clock we cannot guarantee a table up or down because we do not know what will be free. . . . Can you also listen to me? . . . Let me explain to you how a restaurant works. We cannot keep a table empty from seven to nine with the expectation that we must have it available for two at nine o'clock. We must give you what becomes available." The woman cut him off again and he listened again for a long time until he said, "Fine, madame. Good-bye."

"She said I do not know how to run a restaurant," André told me. Surprisingly, he didn't seem perturbed. He shrugged and said, "I give my blood for this restaurant. We all do [meaning his staff]. But there comes a certain time when you say the heck with it."

There are other customer complaints. "People say that the new customers here are not treated the same as regulars," says André. (Forty percent of Lutèce's customers dine there at least five times a year.) "We try to treat everyone the same, but sometimes you can't help it. It's like if you see a schoolmate on the street, you'll hug him, whereas you won't hug a stranger. I'm more careful, but if my staff see someone once a month for over twenty years and this customer comes in, when they say hello it's more from their heart. A new customer pays the same thing as an old customer, I know, but there is the human factor involved. These are people working, not machines. Then there's the question that shouldn't be but is— if the waiter knows he will be tipped well, he will expend a little more.

"Some customers smile at you and you want to serve them. Others come here with the attitude 'Show me what you can do for me.' That puts you, sometimes, in trouble. Today waiters are treated like domestics. Until the attitude of the customers changes, until they treat the waiters more like professionals, service will always be a problem."

And it can be a problem. "When we get complaints from customers, they are rarely about food but always about service. We get letters saying, 'We didn't get a second roll' or 'My glass wasn't refilled.' Big deal! Why didn't they ask for it?"

In conversation André makes light of these omissions, but if he or his wife ever witnessed any mistakes in service, the offending busboy or waiter would be immediately reprimanded.

The service at Lutèce that I witnessed was efficient and professional. The only gaffe I saw was made by a captain who invariably said to tables of more than two, "Who is the host here?" This flustered everyone, from a table of Japanese executives to a group of middle-aged women celebrating a birthday. The Japanese men looked bewildered; the women laughed and pointed their fingers at each other.

What some customers may perceive as a cool reception, I perceived as professionalism. I, for one, don't want a captain or waiter to settle in for a long chat or treat me like his long-lost college roommate. Even after I came to know some of the waiters and captains very well, they maintained a professional distance when I dined there, revealing our acquaintance only by a raised eyebrow or a discreet wink. Only the waiters and captains serving our table approached us—none of the others even came close. At first I was surprised by their distant behavior, but then I realized that while I might be there for pleasure, the Lutèce staff were working and they were taking their jobs very seriously.

Even before my acquaintance with the service staff, there was a moment in my earlier experience of Lutèce that made me understand one of the reasons why the service here rates four stars, and it had nothing to do with the arrival of my courses at the perfect time, or getting a second roll, or having my water glass refilled. It had to do with a captain who unobtrusively rescued me from an unpleasant situation.

I was having lunch alone and a man sitting with three other people across the room kept staring at me. Nonstop. The first time he caught my eye he smiled and, politely, I smiled back. The second time he smiled again. I didn't. Then, time after time, whenever I looked up from my meal, he raised his eyebrows or winked or smiled. I pretended I didn't notice but became more and more uncomfortable and enjoyed my meal less and less. The captain for my station (the set of tables at which I was sitting and over which he was in charge) noticed what was happening and slowly walked over and stood between our two tables, blocking this man's sight of me and allowing me to eat in peace. Whenever the captain wasn't waiting on a table he nonchalantly, without looking at me or the man, returned to this same spot in front of me. He appeared to be standing guard over his station. In reality he was standing guard over a female customer who was being harassed.

It's little things like this—the ability of the staff to sense what is happening in the dining room, and who is and is not happy—that determine whether or not someone has an enjoyable experience in a restaurant.

While the little things are important, the vital secret ingredient behind Lutèce's success is André Soltner himself. There is a freshness, an ingenuousness, to this man that is hard to describe to anyone who hasn't met him. There is happiness, too—his brown eyes are rimmed with crinkly laugh lines, and although his silver hair is thinning and his hairline has receded, his wide forehead is almost unwrinkled. During every meal he will personally recommend dishes and take the orders from customers he knows and, when possible, ask every group of people if they enjoyed their food. This may seem no big deal, but what is special is that he really cares about the answers. This is a man who genuinely loves what he is doing, and his energy, his will to please, and his enthusiasm are infectious.

"I know of no [chef or restaurant owner] who brings more enthusiasm to his work than André Soltner," says Thomas Kelly, director of inspections for the American Express Distinguished Restaurants Program and a restaurant professor at Cornell University's School of Hotel and Restaurant Management. Every year, Kelly and his graduate students make the four-and-a-half-hour trip to Manhattan to talk to André and to eat at Lutèce.

"He comes to work every day as if it was his first day at work. You have to meet the man and experience it to believe it," says Kelly. "He's worth the trip from Cornell just to interact with that, to have a sense of the amount of effort and fortitude he's brought to his job. Among all the other things André does well, he does one thing extraordinarily well, and that's make people happy, and unless you make people happy you aren't going to make a profit.

"He goes table to table to look in your eyes. You can't teach that in a classroom. That's why I bring them to New York. You can't replicate André Soltner in a textbook. [He's] why it's such an excellent restaurant."

Many of André's regular customers and most restaurant critics agree. For example, in its 1988 four-star review of Lutèce, *The New York Times* wrote that much of the restaurant's "appeal centers on Soltner himself, the affable self-effacing host who wouldn't leave his cherished restaurant unless under subpoena."

Michael Maher, managing director of a brokerage firm, who has been patronizing Lutèce for more than twenty years, says, "André is the most important reason I like it here." Only then does he follow up with, "And the service and food are by far the best in the city."

André, eternally youthful in his enthusiasm, inspires the same loyalty in his staff. He is surrounded by people who are totally devoted to him and whom he can fully trust to fulfill the responsibilities that have been delegated to them. Of course the fact that everyone who works for him, with the exception of the unionized dining-room staff, has a share in the profit of his enterprise doesn't hurt his popularity. The dining-room staff was unionized when the restaurant first opened. The kitchen staff, which in the early sixties consisted of André and one assistant, was not interested in joining the union and remains nonunion to this day.

Trust in his staff allows him to ignore areas of the restaurant business that do not interest him. Ask him about food costs and he'll tell you to talk to his accountant. Ask him what licenses the restaurant needs and he's hard-pressed for an answer; a secretary renews them. But he can recite the name of every supplier to you and can tell you anything you want to know about his kitchen. And he knows all of his regular customers by name and makes a point of taking their orders on each visit.

Only once, in the entire twenty years he's been sole owner of the restaurant, has André not been there while a meal was being served. He left on a Friday evening in 1990 and flew to Alsace to attend a gastronomic event during which he was to conduct a cooking demonstration and receive an award. He was conflicted about whether or not to go, but the gathering meant a lot to him because it was to take place in the region where he grew up, and in the end he decided to attend.

But the experience was not a happy one. To start, "I was sick like a dog," says André. "I had an inflammation of the prostate. I thought I was going to die. My doctor said, 'André, you cannot go,' but I said, 'Whatever happens, I go.' "

That Friday, despite his pain, he presided over the kitchen at Lutèce. (In all the years André has been working he has never once called in sick, and he expects the same stoicism and devotion to duty from his staff. "If one is out sick, then it makes everything harder for the others," he says.) He worked until it was time for him to hurry to catch a 10:00 P.M. flight.

He did not enjoy the flight to France. Not only was he in pain but he was doing something that went against the very core of his nature: He was relinquishing control of his restaurant. It was only for a few meals, but still, André worried, you never knew what could go wrong during those meals or during the time between them.

He worried and worried and, sure enough, when he called Simone the following day, his wife told him there had been a fire at the restaurant. "Once I am not there and we had a fire," he says, ruefully shaking his head.

"It started during the night in the boiler in the downstairs kitchen. My wife was sleeping alone upstairs. On Saturday Bill [one of the senior assistant chefs] came to work at four o'clock in the morning. Everything was smoking and there were flames. All my chefs' coats got burned but the fire didn't catch more than that. But [if Bill hadn't arrived early] the whole building could have gone up."

André took this near-tragedy as an omen and from then on has not left the premises during business hours. And anyway, he says, "if I'm not there something is missing. It would be like going to the theater and seeing the understudy instead of the actor you expected. Some restaurateurs try to do it differently but I don't know any examples of where it works too much. If you're not very involved with the restaurant, forget it."

Since André is always at the restaurant during mealtimes, he has little chance to go out to eat himself, to check out what his competition is doing, or simply to enjoy himself. "Restaurant people are different from normal people," he explains. "Most people finish work at five P.M. They can go home and plan to go to the theater. We are like circus people, who are friends among themselves because they work so many hours." A typical workday for André begins at nine in the morning and ends at one the next morning, six days a week. In the summer the restaurant is closed on weekends after Memorial Day and shuts down completely from the last Thursday in July until two days after Labor Day. It is also closed for a week in February.

The Soltners spend most of their summer vacation in France, and it is then that they go to as many restaurants as possible. André's avoidance of New York restaurants seems to have been a blessing in disguise, for unlike other restaurateurs, he has avoided trendiness. To the chagrin of many food critics, who are always searching for new things to write about, Lutèce always has served and, for as long as André is alive, always will serve traditional French food. The only trend André makes allowance for is the one toward healthy eating. If customers ask for it, he will happily grill them a piece of plain fish or leave off a rich sauce. But otherwise, cream and butter reign.

The Soltners' February vacation is spent at their ski house at Hunter Mountain, in upstate New York, as are Sundays, the only full day off they have each week. They leave Lutèce at one on Sunday morning, after Saturday night dinner is over, and arrive at their house at around three-thirty. Even though he gets to bed late, André is always up by nine the next morning.

"In life you have to have something else so you don't go completely crazy on one thing," he says. "My thing is cooking, and I like to have one day that doesn't have anything to do with the restaurant." An active man, he chooses to spend that day outdoors —skiing and chopping wood in the winter, playing tennis, swimming, or bicycling in the summer. "I am a terrible tennis player but I enjoy it so much," he says.

When the weather's bad he putters around the house, fixing whatever needs fixing. Or he'll leaf through one of the hundreds of cookbooks he owns. "I look through them all the time," he says. "For my pleasure or to get an idea or to unwind." He also peruses food magazines. "I get them all," he says. "Everything."

He wouldn't even consider sitting down long enough to watch TV or read a novel. "I would like to read more but I don't have time. I have only one day off and so I want to do everything. Simone is always a little mad with me because she says, 'Can you not relax? You never relax,' and I always say, 'No. No. I want to do all these things.' "

Although André tries to forget about the restaurant on Sundays, he never forgets about cooking and frequently entertains other members of the food world, such as Sirio Maccione, owner of Le Cirque; Gerard Gallian, for twenty-two years owner of the now-defunct Le Cygne; *New York Times* food writer Pierre Franey; and Marc Sarrazin, a partner in DeBragga and Spitler, the company that supplies Lutèce with the bulk of its meat.

Just as André's regular customers do when they talk about Lutèce, Maccione and Franey, when they reminisce about their visits to André's house, focus less on the food André prepared for them than on the man himself. Franey, whose friendship with André developed over skiing at Hunter Mountain, calls André a "solid" person.

"I met André when I was chef at Le Pavillon. When I left Le Pavillon in the sixties and went to work for the Howard Johnson Company, I was criticized because I was switching from a great place to a very ordinary place. Some people switched their ticket about me, but André was all the way with me. André was always the same. He was always there and I was very grateful for that.

"André wasn't influenced by people, the press, or the trends of the day," Franey continues. "He's solid like the Rock of Gibraltar. André is still going to be André no matter what people say. He's straight, no baloney. He's cooking his best on classical cooking. He's not influenced by nouvelle cuisine, by the new things that are going on. He's very, very solid. [And] he's a great human being. He loves people. He's very sympathetic and is always helping young people."

In fact, one of the people André helped get established in the restaurant world is Le Cirque's Maccione, who today also has a house at Hunter Mountain and considers André one of his best friends. "I got close to him when I started to think about opening my restaurant about twenty years ago," says Maccione. "He always found the time to talk to me about it. He was always very nice. At one point I had a big problem. I had a partner who was a chef and he retired. I had to find a chef. He found me a chef and he helped me in other ways in the beginning when we really needed it."

He also helped Maccione's three sons learn how to ski. For the past fifteen years the Macciones have spent Christmas Eve at the Soltners' house and the Soltners have spent New Year's Day at the Maccione home.

"He would prepare the real food," says Maccione. "We always start with caviar. Both our cultures require that. Then we would have fish or soup and rack of lamb. A couple of times we've had choucroute. He does classical French, and it's always very, very good."

Remembering André's choucroute, Franey says, "In this choucroute he had little meatballs made with pork and caraway seeds. It was so delicious that even today I can taste the choucroute with all the sausages and smoked pork. He has a sense of taste—that's what makes a great chef."

And that's what André is, first and foremost. Ask him to describe himself and the first words out of his mouth are "I am a cook."

This single-mindedness never abates on Sundays. Although André welcomes the break from the operational and administrative end of the restaurant, he never stops thinking about cooking. "On the weekend I have more time to think," he says. "I do a lot of thinking about food—new dishes that I can do. Cooking is my joy, and on the ski lift I'll think of something I can make, or I'll create in the car, or when I sleep."

★　★　★　★

And so, for now, let us leave André and his wife asleep in the unassuming brownstone on New York City's East Fiftieth Street that shelters every aspect of their lives. From afar, the building looks like a residence. Up close, only a discreet furled awning and a small plaque by the door reveal that this building is also home to the world-famous Lutèce.

Farther up the street Jacques Coustar, who has worked for André off and on since 1956, when they were both young chefs in Paris, and who is one of Lutèce's three *sous-chefs* (senior assistant chefs), is hurrying toward the restaurant. A short, serious man with a mustache, a full head of wispy, baby-fine dark gray hair, and square wire-frame glasses, Jacques woke at four-fifteen, dressed, and was at the subway stop in working-class Maspeth, Queens, at four-fifty. You'd think the train would be empty at that hour but it's usually filled with other restaurant, hotel, and factory workers on their way to work. "And bums are lying all over the seats," says Jacques, his perfect English laced with a slight French accent. "I always stand up on the train. And it stinks. It's disgusting."

On the subway, Jacques often runs into the chef for the management dining room at *The New York Times,* and to pass the time and help each other ignore the ugliness and misery of the homeless people sleeping nearby, they talk about their gardens. The *Times* chef has a weekend house in Pennsylvania; Jacques has a little vegetable-and-herb garden in his backyard in Queens. Their talk of gardening evokes images of fresh green sprouts, bright tomatoes dripping with dew, and the earthy smell of just-watered soil, all of which help them block out the stench of urine surrounding them on the subway. Their talk also keeps them from contemplating the lives of those who eat only what is handed out to them or what they find in garbage cans. These homeless people only peripherally touch Jacques's existence. On the subway they may be unavoidable, and out on the street at this hour anarchy may prevail, with garbage trucks running red lights and driving up deserted one-way streets the wrong way, screeching and whining as they go, but Jacques knows that once he gets inside Lutèce, all will be orderly, all will be good.

This goodness is protected by secure locks and an alarm system, which Jacques deactivates. He enters through the front door, turns right into the tiny bar area—crowded with just four round tables—

and then turns left, heading down a long hallway. At the end of the hallway is the main dining room. Behind the hallway's long right-hand wall is the kitchen, one end of which will be his domain for the next eight hours. But before he can settle here, he must go through the series of duties he performs six mornings a week.

Jacques walks into the long, narrow kitchen, flicks on the lights, and turns right, into the area where he works. He turns on the gas to the three stoves, two overhead broilers, two large ovens, and one warming station that stand to his left. As he heads back for the door, his eyes take in the spic-and-span condition in which last night's dinner crew left the small kitchen. The metal counters and refrigerators and the red clay tile floor shine, and the big butcher-block chopping areas are perfectly clean.

Jacques walks back toward the restaurant's entrance and runs up the staircase to the second floor. In the hall connecting the two small upstairs dining rooms, he turns on the exhaust fan that will carry all cooking smells directly outside, keeping the air in the dining areas fresh and clean.

Back downstairs, he walks through another door directly across from the entrance to the kitchen. It opens onto a steep staircase that takes him down to the prep kitchen, which consists of two rooms. The smaller of the two holds a little two-burner stove, a smoker, an ice-cream maker, a huge pressure cooker (in which veal stock has been simmering overnight), a walk-in refrigerator for white wine, champagne, and flower arrangements, and a chest-level oven and steamer called a Rational Combi-Oven/Steamer. First introduced in 1987, the oven can function as a dry cooking oven, a steamer, or a combination convection oven and steamer for high-humidity roasting and baking. This oven roasts meats without drying them and in doing so helps the restaurant make money: The higher humidity inhibits the evaporation of the natural juices in meat, so there is less loss from shrinkage—and more potential for profit. André was so impressed with the oven that he endorsed it gratis (though he did get an $8,000 oven for free).

Jacques turns on the lights in the first room and unlocks the door to the adjoining, larger room. It is here that the meat is butchered, the fish filleted, the vegetables chopped, and the desserts and most entrées assembled. After turning on the lights here too, he checks the thermostat outside the walk-in refrigerator, confirming that the temperature is within the proper range, thirty-four to thirty-six degrees. Next, he opens the doors to the two small refrigerators and six freezers located under the counters that line the far end of the room and makes sure they are working.

He then returns to the smaller room and heads for the back, where each of the cooks has a locker to store his (they are indeed all male) personal belongings. Jacques changes into the working uniform of most restaurants: black-and-white checked pants (checked so that spots don't show as readily) and a white long-sleeved shirt-jacket (white to deflect heat; long-sleeved to protect against burns). He ties a knee-length white apron around his waist and a white kerchief around his neck. (The kerchief keeps sweat from pouring down the cooks' backs.) He won't put on the final part of the uniform—a tall white paper toque—until customers begin to arrive.

Only now that he's officially dressed for the day does Jacques check on the veal stock he put on to simmer yesterday afternoon at around four o'clock, which will be ready this morning at ten-thirty. This stock is used as a base for almost all the sauces served here. Jacques lifts the cover of the pressure cooker and gives the simmering liquid a stir with a huge ladle, rearranging the browned bones and vegetables before replacing the cover.

That done, he heads back to the larger room and lays out four stainless steel trays on the counter outside the refrigerator. He walks into the refrigerator and, oblivious to the chill, takes out white plastic buckets filled with vegetables he chopped yesterday for the soups, sauces, and venison stew he's about to start cooking upstairs. Besides making all the soups, most of the sauces, and the stews in advance, Jacques also cooks meats and poultry during lunch service and makes lunch for the staff of forty-two.

Jacques places all of these buckets on one tray. He loads the other trays with leftover chicken stock, consommé; fish soup and pea soup; milk; cream; butter; spaetzle; long noodles; crab meat; and whole onions, morels, and parsley.

These trays are too heavy for Jacques to carry and he leaves them there for Guido Torres—a cleaning man, potwasher, and general kitchen helper who will be arriving momentarily—to carry upstairs for him.

Jacques returns to the upstairs kitchen and walks down the narrow aisle with the stoves and ovens on the left side and a counter covered with two large wooden chopping boards on the right. Under this counter are two refrigerators and one freezer. The refrigerators are stocked with ingredients and garnishes Jacques will be using for the meats and poultry he cooks during lunch service.

Jacques opens the refrigerators and takes out their contents—string beans, sliced mushrooms, tomatoes, lemon juice, cream, and so forth. He wipes down the inside of the refrigerators and then puts everything back. "Everything always goes in the same place," he says, "so that I can reach them fast during service. I don't even have to look. I just put in my hand and grab what I need. If you lose time looking for your stuff, forget it." During lunch service these refrigerators will also hold fish, meat, and chicken but at this time of day, those items are either still in the downstairs walk-in refrigerator or about to be delivered.

Just as Jacques finishes straightening up, Guido, the kitchen aide, dressed in the same type of work clothes as Jacques, brings up the trays and Jacques begins work on the sauces he will make today.

These sauces are the basis of French cuisine, and Jacques learned to make them at a very young age. He began his apprenticeship at fourteen, not out of a desire to be a chef but to earn money. "I come from a very poor family," he says. "My father had a little garage in a little town in France and it was tough to find a job. We knew of this hotel near our house and my father asked if they had an opening for me. A year later they did."

Jacques signed on for a three-year apprenticeship in 1952. After it was completed, he went to Paris, and it was there, at Chez

Hansi, that he first worked for André. Jacques came to New York and Lutèce in 1963. In 1969 he met and married French-born Mirielle, who now works the coat check at Lutèce during lunch service.

But Jacques's tenure at Lutèce was not unbroken. In 1976 he, Mirielle, and their two daughters moved to France and opened a restaurant called Au Petit Cheminot in Tours.

Owning a restaurant is the ultimate dream of most chefs, and Jacques thought that this little place, which served only one dish to one hundred customers a day, was the fulfillment of that dream. "My wife and I put everything we had into it. I did the kitchen and she was the cashier and bartender at the same time."

But "everything" proved to be too much, especially for Mirielle. Says Jacques: "After five years my wife said the restaurant was too tough. She was so tired all the time. She said, 'I don't want to kill myself. It's too hard. We can't enjoy life.' "

And so they hired a manager to run the restaurant for them and returned to New York in 1981. Jacques cooked at La Côte Basque and at another restaurant, which he prefers not to name because the owner fired him after six years, owing to a disagreement over a promised partnership that never materialized. Jacques then went to work briefly in the management dining room at the New York headquarters of First Boston Bank. Mirielle got a job checking coats at Lutèce, and Jacques would come and meet her there after work. When a *sous-chef* position opened up at Lutèce in 1986, André offered it to Jacques, and he accepted.

Given a choice, Jacques would prefer to be working at his own place, but his wife's happiness was important to him, and so here he is. The benefit of working for someone else, of course, is that when the workday is over, Jacques is able to forget about the restaurant. But André can't.

★ ★ ★ ★

André was born on November 20, 1932, in a small town called Thann in Alsace, France, on the French-German border. He was the second son of a carpenter father and a mother who was a good cook. From early childhood, André loved to watch his mother prepare meals. "I was always on a stool or on a chair, looking at how she did it and then trying it myself," he says.

But he also liked to watch his father work, and if he had been able to, he would have become a carpenter, "because it's a very creative business. I very often worked with my father when I wasn't in school and I liked it very much." But, as was the way in those days, the business was passed on to the eldest son, and so André decided to apprentice to become a cook.

"I dreamed to be a great chef who would one day have my own restaurant," he says. "I was very ambitious. I was born like that. But it wasn't only with cooking that I was ambitious. I was a boy scout, and you have, you know, the badges and I wanted to have the most badges of our group. I went skiing when I was a kid and I hoped to be the fastest. It is in my character."

The Hôtel du Parc was the major hotel in the area, and when André was fourteen, his father took him there to inquire about apprenticeship openings. There were none, but the chef said he would keep the boy in mind. In the meantime, André was accepted at another restaurant in the nearby town of Colmar. "I didn't like it," says André. "I had a tough time there. They were not so warm and I was this young guy. One day I just escaped at five o'clock in the morning. I took my suitcase and escaped and went home." Soon there was an opening at the Hôtel du Parc, where André happily completed his three-year apprenticeship.

"That was tough too, but I loved it. The feeling was warmer, so I didn't mind working a lot of hours. As soon as my father signed the papers, the chef looked at me and said, 'Now you belong to me,' and he wasn't kidding." For a dollar a month to start, plus room and board, André assisted in every station of the kitchen.

He worked six days a week, starting at seven-thirty in the morning and ending at nine at night. Two afternoons a week, Mondays and Tuesdays, he also went to school from three to five-thirty to learn the business aspects of running a restaurant, such as how to calculate food and labor costs and to keep accounts.

"On school days we started at seven-thirty in the morning,

worked until two, ran to school, were in school, and then ran back to the restaurant," says André. "Normally we started working on dinner at five, but on our school days we were allowed to come in later. But the chef was always mad at us. He always said we took too much time to get to work from school, and there was a fight every time, so we always had to run.

"Apprenticeship was very tough on a young guy. I think I realize more today how tough it was than I did when I was there. We worked every day a lot, and I remember when I was there my only thing besides work was Sunday evening, when my friend and I went to a café with live music and we had one beer. We certainly were not spoiled kids. But I was quite happy. I had a good life. The chef was nice and so were all the *sous-chefs*. I was Bubby there. They called me Bubby because I was very small, a small, small kid."

A small kid with a great love of food and a big appetite—which the chef decided to get under control from the very beginning. "One day," says André, "the pastry chef made *éclairs au chocolat*. My chef said, 'Bubby, take one.' When you are a child . . . because, you know, we were children—fourteen. He gave me one and oh! it was fantastic. And he gave me a second one and then he said, 'Take one more.' Then the *saucier* said, 'You should have an éclair.' They stuffed me with these éclairs. It was fantastic but I got sick and up to this day I cannot eat *éclairs au chocolat*. They used to do that [in apprenticeship], to stuff you like that so that you don't go to pick at the food all the time."

On the whole, André says, apprenticeship was "a good school for later. The chef worked six days a week. He was the first one in the kitchen and, besides the apprentices, the last one who left. He was very dedicated to his work and he wasn't paid so well. He was tough. Very tough. I loved him, the guy. He kicked or slapped us when we did something wrong. It's not like today when that's a catastrophe. 'It's okay,' my parents said to him. He didn't kill us but if we did something wrong he gave us one very easy. So it was on us to have enough distance between him and us so that he could not get us. He didn't hit us every day, you know, *boom*.

When he did sometimes—*bang,* he gave you one because you overcooked or burned something—then you'd stay in your corner and sulk, so the next day he said, 'You feel better? On your day off you come have lunch with me and my family.' The apprentices and cooks each had a different day off and mine was Thursday, the same as his. It's not a big thing, but when you are an apprentice and you see this guy like God and he invites you to his home for lunch, it's very special. When I looked at my chef I thought, Wow. The chef. That's something. I thought that one day everyone would call me chef. I was very impressed by that."

As a young boy André also dreamed that one day he would win the Meilleur Ouvrier de France, the highest award for craftsmanship in various fields given by the French government. "I thought maybe it would not be possible but I remember it was in my head already," he says of the treasured award he won in 1968.

In André's second year of apprenticeship, his salary was raised to two dollars a month, and then a fortuitous late-night visit by a group of hunters resulted in the tripling of his salary. "Our kitchen closed more or less at nine o'clock but there were always customers longer than nine o'clock, so that every night one of the three apprentices stayed until ten or ten-thirty to send the last desserts out, clean up, and to finish in the kitchen," says André. "In my second year I was the one closing the kitchen. The boss of the hotel was a hunter. A few of his hunting companions came in at nine forty-five and they wanted to eat. The boss came down then to see who was in the kitchen, but all the chefs had left at nine o'clock. He said, 'Bubby, I have some people here to feed. Is the chef gone?' and I said yes and he said, 'Oh, my God, what do I do? What do we do? They want to eat.' I said, 'Well, I think I can do it.' I made trout for these ten hunters and apparently they liked it very much.

"The next day the boss was very excited, very pleased. He called my chef and told him, 'We had this big party. Everybody was gone and Bubby cooked for us and it was great.' The chef decided to give me three thousand francs from then on, so I had six dollars a month. That helped me a lot. This was my only income. From the time I left home at fourteen I was, my whole life, completely on my own. My parents never helped to give me anything. They didn't have to take care of me at all. I never went home and said, 'I need something. I need money.' Then when I had the six dollars I was making enough money to put some away on the side. If you have room and board you don't need too much. And we had to work. We didn't have time to go to the movies or whatever."

Cooking was André's life and by the third year of his apprenticeship he was already beginning to feel that he was better than the average Pierre. He entered a food show and "made a very nice exposition and my plate was very much looked at. People would say, 'Oh, he's still an apprentice. Look what he did.' Then I was already a little bit recognized, more than average."

He got even more recognition when, upon completing his apprenticeship, he took the two-day certification exam required for professional cooks in France and received the highest possible grade. He then worked, during the summer 1951 season, at the Hôtel Royale in Deauville as a *commis,* or assistant *saucier,* helping the chef who made the sauces for the restaurant. In the winter he went back to Alsace, to the Hôtel Europe in Saint Louis, where he was also an assistant. On his day off he skied, a sport he loves to this day.

The following summer he moved to the Palace Hotel in Pontresina, Switzerland, as *entremettier,* the chef in charge of the vegetables and the soups. In the winter he went to Hotel Acker in eastern Switzerland, where he had to sign a contract promising he would not ski. "If you break a leg you cannot work," André explains. "It's a loss for them in the middle of the season. So I signed the contract, went skiing, and broke my leg. I had no insurance because of that. Switzerland is very strict. I had to pay for my hospital [because he had broken his contract]. The little money I had then all went to the hospital."

In the summer he returned to the Palace Hotel. That fall he was drafted into the French army and didn't tell his superiors that he was a cook. "I would have been taken off the skis and put into the kitchen." Instead, he told them he was a carpenter, and he was placed in the Alpine troops. "I spent the first six months in the Alps in France. That was great, skiing every day." When the Algerian revolt against French rule began in the summer of 1954, André's regiment was sent to neighboring Tunisia, "in the mountains there, for nine months. We didn't do too much, except waiting. We were there in case anything happened in Tunisia but we didn't do any fighting."

When André was released from the army in April 1955 he began working at Chez Hansi, an Alsatian restaurant in Paris, as "the round man." The restaurant was open every day, and six days a week André changed posts, replacing whichever cook was off. In time he became *sous-chef* and then, in 1959, at the age of twenty-six, he became the chef, with fourteen cooks and two pastry chefs reporting to him. "I was very young and I was maybe not the best chef but I was the chef."

That same year André entered a culinary show near Paris. "The first time I entered I was unknown in Paris but I get the bronze medal," says André. "I was a little recognized by other chefs then. The year after that I get the gold medal. For the chefs I was then starting to be more in the limelight."

Meanwhile in the United States French cuisine was expanding its own place in the limelight. The superb restaurant in the French pavilion of the 1939 and 1940 New York World's Fair had introduced Americans to this cuisine. The restaurant was run by the great maître d' Henri Soulé, and after the fair was over, Soulé moved his establishment to East Fifty-fifth Street and called it Le Pavillon, in memory of the pavilion.

In the years that followed, Le Pavillon became a New York landmark, consistently garnering four-star reviews and training a whole series of chefs and waiters who went on to found their own restaurants—places such as La Caravelle and La Grenouille. One of Le Pavillon's biggest fans in the late fifties was a young New Yorker who was such a Francophile that he changed his name from Andrew Sussman to André Surmain. He was in the airline catering business but he had a dream: to go Le Pavillon one better and to open the best, most expensive, most exclusive French restaurant in Manhattan.

He decided to open the restaurant on the downstairs floors of his home on East Fiftieth Street and began looking for a young chef, someone who wouldn't require a high salary but who was full of promise. One of the pastry chefs who worked for Surmain had once worked for André at Chez Hansi and told Surmain about him.

Surmain went to Paris, had lunch at Chez Hansi, and told the maître d' he had greetings for André from the pastry chef. After lunch service was finished, André went over to Surmain's table "to say hello to this American guy who brought me greetings." Surmain told André he'd like to talk to him outside the restaurant and the two arranged to meet the following day at a hotel. It was there that Surmain told him all about his grandiose plans and offered André the chef's position. At the time André was making ninety-five dollars a month. Surmain offered to match that salary and also told him he would make him a partner if things worked out.

"My mother's father had been a gold digger in Nevada for a few years," says André. "He came back to France to serve in the army, thinking he'd go back to America, which he loved. But he met my grandmother and decided to stay in France. But he never forgot America, and in my childhood I had my head full of Nevada and Indians and California and how great America was. For us Europeans then, America was paradise. I thought [Surmain's offer] over a little bit, and I thought since I didn't speak English, going to New York would be a very good way for me to learn. I was twenty-eight and I said, 'What do I have to lose? Let's go.' " And so he went, leaving behind Simone, whom he'd met while she was a waitress at Chez Hansi and whom he had been dating.

Lutèce—whose name comes from "Lutetia," the ancient name of Paris—opened on February 16, 1961. As Surmain had planned, it was the city's most lavishly decorated and expensive restaurant, with a lunch price-fixed at $8.50. "But everybody was so outraged and screaming that it was a scandal that he was charging so much that he went down to six dollars and fifty cents and charged eight twenty-five for the à la carte main courses at dinner," says André. (To give you a basis of comparison, back then the restaurant was paying $1.75 apiece for Baccarat crystal glasses. Today the same glasses would cost around $110.00 each. Because crystal is so expensive, the restaurant today uses glass instead.)

To put it mildly, Lutèce was not an immediate success. In a review written one month after it opened, Craig Claiborne, then the restaurant critic for *The New York Times,* said that although the foie gras in brioche loaf and roast veal with truffled kidneys were superb, "the food at Lutèce could not be called great cuisine."

And now? Thirty-one years later, asked if he would consider the food at Lutèce "great cuisine," Claiborne says, "I would indeed." Claiborne, who has retired from *The New York Times,* adds that what makes cuisine great is "very difficult to pinpoint. It's a reflection of the chef's inspiration but it's impossible to define in a brief space." He calls Lutèce "one of the finest French restaurants in the city and, to my taste, one of the best restaurants in America. All of the essential elements of a fine restaurant are a part of Lutèce."

But it wasn't just the lack of great cuisine that kept the crowds away. Surmain's snobbery was another problem. He turned away people who lacked the proper social finish or whose clothing he didn't like.

"We really didn't do too well, and after two years I said, 'I'm wasting my time here,' " recalls André. " 'I quit.' And Surmain said, 'No, you can't leave. We are doing a little better now. And what about your partnership?' and I said, 'You haven't mentioned it again.' " So after some negotiating, André became a 30 percent partner.

The first thing he did as a partner was to make sure that all the suppliers were paid promptly. "André [Surmain] and me are two different types of guys," says André. "He feels very comfortable with debts and I feel very uncomfortable. In business, when you owe money, you cannot go to the supplier and ask him for the best if you don't pay him."

To this day André uses the fact that he is a prompt bill-payer as leverage with his suppliers. Ariane Daguin, co-owner of D'Artagnan, Inc., Lutèce's poultry, game, and foie gras supplier, says that when André calls to place an order he starts the conversation by simply saying, "Hello." But if there's a problem with a delivery, the first words out of his mouth are "Don't I pay my bills?"

By the time André and Surmain became partners, André and Simone were already married. The ceremony took place in France in 1962. André returned to New York alone, but as soon as Simone got her immigration papers, in July 1963, she came to join him. She immediately went to work at Lutèce, splitting the cashier duties with Surmain's wife while Surmain acted as host.

André and Simone lived around the corner from the restaurant while Surmain and his family lived above it. Surmain had four children, and his living quarters were much too small for his family. In 1965 the Surmains and the Soltners switched buildings, with Surmain taking a large apartment in the Soltners' old building and André and Simone moving into the apartment above Lutèce, where they were destined to remain.

Also in 1965, the Soltners bought their first car, a Volkswagen Beetle. Every Sunday they'd take a drive, either out to Long Island or upstate. It was on one of those drives that André discovered that there was skiing close to New York, a fact he'd never known. One winter day they stumbled across a small ski area called Silver Mine, now defunct. "We stopped there and saw people skiing," André recalls. "Simone comes from Normandy. She didn't know what snow was. I said I was very good at skiing. I was wearing a blue suit that day, and Simone, who didn't know what's what, said, 'Why are you not going?' I said, 'I am in a suit,' and she said, 'So what?' and I said, 'You're right. So what?'

"So I rented skis and boots, and, in my blue suit, I went up with the little ski lift and came down. I didn't have skis on in twelve years, but it's like bicycling. You don't forget. I said, 'My God! I ski like before!' We came back and the next day, Monday, I went to Herman's and bought a pair of skis and boots and ski clothes. From there on we went skiing every Sunday."

In 1968 André traveled to France to compete for his cherished Meilleur Ouvrier de France. The award honors technical skills and the taste of the final dishes, rather than creativity. All of the contestants have to prepare the same dishes, chosen by the award committee. The contest starts regionally and the finals are in Paris.

During the year André competed, all the contestants had to prepare *sole à la catalane* as the appetizer, *poularde chevalière* as the entrée, and chocolate soufflé for eight people for dessert. The first dish—poached tomatoes stuffed with fillet of sole and served with beurre blanc—is still sometimes offered as a special at Lutèce.

The entrée did not share the same longevity. "I think it was a terrible recipe," André says of the chicken. "Disgusting." So disgusting that he hates even to talk about what exactly it involved but when pressed he says, "It's a very technical dish, very classic and old. Escoffier developed the recipe. You need a lot of dexterity because there are a lot of things going on. You poach the chicken. Then you cut into it and put in truffles. Then with the cockscomb you make quenelles [dumplings]. Disgusting." He makes a face like a little kid being forced to swallow his medicine.

The trick behind the dessert was to get the soufflé to rise straight, without dipping in the middle. "A small soufflé is okay to make," says André. "One for eight people is hard."

In spite of his feelings about the chicken, André executed the three dishes flawlessly and won the award. "Winning is the thing that pleased me the most professionally," he says.

Business at Lutèce, helped along by the publicity generated by this award, continued to grow. Confident about the restaurant's success, the Soltners bought property at Hunter Mountain in 1969, and built their first ski house there. Then in 1972 the two partners started having what André calls "different philosophies."

"I believe in hard work and in always being here," he says. "Surmain saw it differently. He sailed across the Atlantic, had a car collection, and a farm in Majorca. He wasn't here for much of the time.

"I decided it wasn't fair that I was working so hard and he

wasn't, and I decided to leave," says André. "My partner said, 'What, are you kidding? I'm so sick of this business. I'll leave.' " And so André became the sole owner.

"When he left I didn't know what would happen," remembers André. "I was a little scared. He was a very public man. He had a lot of people who disliked him but many liked him. He was good with public relations."

Despite André's trepidation, business increased. During his first year as sole owner *The New York Times* wrote, "Anyone who cares seriously about great food should start a special savings account earmarked for meals at this magnificent French restaurant." Other publications followed suit. *Forbes,* for instance, said: "[From Soltner's domain] . . . issues forth dish after dish of imaginative and unquestioned quality. Rarely is anything disappointing."

"When [my partner] was here we never hit one hundred dinners," says André, referring to the number of meals served per night. "Then pretty fast we went to one hundred twenty. I was free to do what I wanted and I made the restaurant more comfortable, not too snobbish. Many people who hadn't come because of his attitude started to come back. We still have the same people. We have everybody eating here, from movie actors to ambassadors, but we leave them alone and don't do too big of a fuss over them and people don't feel too bothered with all these stuffy things. Everybody feels pretty comfortable.

"I am a cook, you know, so it would be ridiculous that I try to have a snobbish restaurant. I am a working man and a cook behind my stove, but it seems that the people like [what I do] very much."

Indeed. Of course, thanks to the current state of the economy, things are not as rosy today as they were in 1987, when reservations had to be made one month in advance. These days you can usually make a reservation the week before the day you want, and often you can get one for the same day.

Today, for instance, tables are still available for lunch and for the six o'clock dinner seating. The eight o'clock seating, the most popular at all restaurants, is booked and includes a private party for nineteen that will be held in one of the upstairs dining rooms.

Lutèce's twenty-nine tables can seat seventy-five people at one time. Today there are sixty confirmed reservations for lunch and one hundred thirty for dinner. That means there are fifteen seats still available for lunch and twenty for the first dinner seating. On fully booked days Lutèce serves ninety for lunch (turning some tables twice) and one hundred sixty for dinner, squeezing in an extra ten people for a third seating.

In six hours Lutèce will be almost full but now, at 6:15 A.M., the four small dining rooms are still empty, the tables stripped of tablecloths and stacked one on top of another.

Let's talk about these dining rooms for a moment. Whenever friends of mine visit Lutèce for the first time, I warn them not to expect much in the way of decor. In fact, the restaurant errs slightly in the other direction. The downstairs dining rooms are perhaps *too* casual, the Lutèce brochures on the table *too* touristy, the ladies' room too similar to what you might find in an impeccably clean gas station, complete with poor lighting and a plastic toilet seat wrapper.

For first-time visitors, especially tourists, the restaurant's plainness can be disappointing. For regular customers, however, its simplicity is a welcome respite from the formality and stiffness of many other restaurants in this league.

Fashion designer Bill Blass, for instance, lives in the neighborhood and says he "uses" Lutèce, one of his favorite restaurants, "as a neighborhood bistro."

"It's not a glamorous-looking place," says Blass. "It's more glamorous from the outside than the inside. But that's not a drawback. Keeping it that way makes it look like it's in a small town in France and it happens to be that particular town's best restaurant. He's managed to escape the New Yorkese glitter. The rooms at Lutèce don't impose on you."

Downstairs there are two dining rooms. The first, for smokers, is very small, with just four tables. There are no windows and not much to enliven it, yet it is here that many longtime customers, including Blass, former president Richard Nixon, and food critic Mimi Sheraton, prefer to sit.

The adjoining second dining room, the main one, is pretty but simple. Once the building's backyard, it is now enclosed but is still meant to look and feel like an outdoor garden. However, with only a few potted palms and two or three roses in bud vases at the tables, it feels more like the inside of a barn, albeit a charming one with an opaque glass ceiling, slate floor, and pink walls fronted by white latticework.

At this time of day, sitting in the first dining room, cleaning man/ kitchen aide Juan Espinal is hand-polishing the silverware. This chore takes him four hours every day and it is a task he's done every workday morning for the past twelve years. After he's finished the silver, he will vacuum the two upstairs dining rooms and then go to work in the downstairs kitchen, where he will help with whatever chopping or cleaning needs to be done.

Guido, who carried Jacques's trays upstairs earlier, as he has every day during the three years he's worked here, has already hosed down the sidewalk outside and is mopping the larger dining room's slate floor. After he's finished he will also assist in the downstairs kitchen, until three-thirty.

Jacques, in the meantime, is busy at his stove, cooking today's special soup, cream of pumpkin. The back of his head is visible through the long, high, narrow window cut into the length of the kitchen wall but his head disappears from view as he bends over, opens one of the refrigerators underneath the counter, takes out an assortment of silver creamers that were on the dining-room tables last night, and pours the leftover cream into a sauce he's making for the staff's lunch.

His cheeks are red from the stove's heat, and I notice a terrible burn on the side of his left wrist. When I ask about it, he says he got it reaching into the oven. "I don't even notice burns anymore," he says. "My daughter will see one and say, 'Oh, my God!' but . . ." He shrugs, implying that burns are all in a day's work. So too is heat. The temperature in front of the stove is so high that as I watch him work, I begin to wonder if my mascara is melting. Whenever Jacques crouches down to pull something out of the refrigerator, I crouch down too, simply to cool off by the open refrigerator door. When I comment on the heat, Jacques says, "You get used to it."

$\mathscr{P}$OTAGE CRÈME ST. GERMAIN

SPLIT PEA SOUP

FOR 8 PEOPLE

$\frac{1}{2}$ lb. split peas

4 Tb unsalted butter
($\frac{1}{2}$ stick)

2 oz. smoked bacon,
diced

1 medium white onion,
sliced

1 leek (the white part
only), washed, cut in
$\frac{1}{4}$-inch slices

1 carrot, trimmed,
peeled, washed, cut in
$\frac{1}{4}$-inch pieces

1 garlic clove, peeled
and crushed

1 bouquet garni (tie a
sprig each of parsley
and thyme and 1 bay
leaf tightly with white
string)

Salt

Pepper, freshly ground

3 slices of white bread,
crusts removed, cut in
$\frac{1}{4}$-inch cubes

$\frac{1}{2}$ cup heavy cream

$\frac{1}{2}$ Tb chervil leaves

Wash the split peas in several changes of cold water. Then soak them in cold water for 2 hours. Drain and set aside.

In a large saucepan, melt 2 tablespoons of the butter. Add the bacon, and sauté over medium heat for 4 minutes. Add the onion, leek, carrot, and garlic, and sauté over low heat for 3 more minutes.

Add the split peas and 1$\frac{1}{2}$ quarts of water. Add the bouquet garni, salt, and pepper. Bring to the boil, and simmer over low heat, covered, for 1$\frac{1}{2}$ hours.

While the soup is simmering, melt the remaining 2 tablespoons of butter in a skillet, and sauté the croutons until they are golden brown. Drain the croutons on a paper towel and set aside.

When the soup has cooked, remove the bouquet garni, puree the soup in a food processor (about 2 minutes), and pass it through a fine sieve. Return the soup to its pot, and bring it to a simmer. Stir in the cream. Add salt and pepper to taste. Sprinkle with the chervil, and serve with the croutons.

6:20 A.M.

A second *sous-chef,* thirty-two-year-old Bill Peet, arrives in jeans and sneakers and walks downstairs to change into his work clothes. Unlike Jacques, who is in charge of the upstairs, or "hot," kitchen—the "hot" referring both to the temperature, since this is where the stoves and all but one of the ovens are located, and to the pressure, since this is where the final cooking of all entrées is done on deadline—Bill is in charge of the downstairs, or "cold," kitchen—the prep kitchen, where the vegetables are peeled and chopped, meat is butchered, desserts made, and entrées assembled to the just-before-cooking stage.

The two kitchens, hot and cold, suit the personalities of the men overseeing them: Jacques is hot, quick to anger at a supplier who doesn't come on time, and always intently working ("Work in the kitchen is never finished," he says. "I have no radio. I never talk to anybody. I have always something to do"). Brown-haired Bill, although not cold, is definitely cool. He stores a radio in a plastic container and tunes it to a rock music station until André comes down to this kitchen, around nine-thirty. Then Bill turns it off because, he says, André "is nervous and he doesn't understand rock and roll. He'll yell, 'Get me rid of this crap!' "

The work upstairs goes on in silence, but the cooks downstairs are perpetually giving each other a hard time about everything, from their hometowns to the use of counter space. This teasing continues all day.

Despite his easygoing manner, Bill, who graduated from the Culinary Institute of America (CIA) in Hyde Park, New York, and has been at Lutèce for eleven years, is quite serious about his work. He's able to make his job look easy, he says, because "I'm very organized."

Bill, who loved food as a kid, spent the first thirteen years of his life in a house near the CIA, where his mother was a secretary to the vice president. This vice president frequently walked Bill through the school. "I was a fat little kid and I was in my glory," says the now-slim Bill, who worked in restaurants throughout high school. After graduating from the CIA he worked at another French restaurant for six months before coming to Lutèce.

Bill began working nights in the *garde manger* station in the upstairs kitchen, filling the orders for cold appetizers, salads, and desserts. He was then promoted to work at the stoves, first sautéing noodles and vegetables and then, after another promotion, cooking the fish dishes.

In 1984 he moved downstairs to oversee the prep kitchen. "It's the best position in the house," he says. "There's play on what you can do down here. You get to see the products and the specials. The new things go on down here." Whereas their customers love the finished product, chefs take pleasure in the raw ingredients. Like fabric to a clothing designer or paint to an artist, raw fish, meats, and produce, to a chef, are what make his or her work possible.

Another reason Bill favors his current position is that he gets to leave at four in the afternoon and spend the evenings with his wife and two young sons. Behind a spice canister at his workstation he has taped a photo of the two adorable boys.

"When I started here I was a bachelor," he says. "Now I'm married and have two kids. I have a lot of responsibilities at home." That is one reason why he has remained at Lutèce for so long. "We have no union in the kitchen but we have great benefits—major medical, dental. Some chefs move from job to job. I can't afford to do that."

He is, however, thinking about doing some catering on the side, "to have a chance to show my own stuff." His ultimate goal is to open his own place, a bed-and-breakfast in upstate New York. "Making a lot of money isn't important to me. I just want a nice life for myself and my kids. My grandmother still lives upstate and whenever I call her she's in the garden. That's the kind of life I'd like."

Bill gardens on the weekends but the closest he gets to a garden during the workday is via contact with the fresh produce that arrives here daily. Although ordering responsibilities are divided among André (meat and fish), Jacques (fruit, vegetables, and dairy), and Bill (staples like spices, flour, sugar, and salt), Bill is the one who checks in all of them. These deliveries will begin arriving any moment.

Dressed now in a white jacket and black-and-white checked pants, Bill checks the "to do" list that André leaves for him each night. The list is always scribbled on a two-by-four-inch piece of white paper and is always left in the same place—pierced onto a tiny nail on the wall at the far left end of the counter that is Bill's workstation.

This counter starts midway along the far left wall and runs to the end of the room. Before the start of the counter is a three-sided open cubicle, bordered on the right by the walk-in refrigerator and on the other two sides by short counters that, as the day unfolds, will be shared by two people. Space—both in this kitchen and the one upstairs—is tight.

This morning both counters in the cubicle will be the domain of Bill's assistant, twenty-four-year-old Joe O'Brien, who will arrive shortly. He too will use André's note as a map to his responsibilities.

As always, this note is simply a list of the dishes that need to be assembled that day. Just by looking at the name of a dish, Bill knows what needs to be done, as would all chefs who have been trained in classical cooking methods.

Today eight dishes are listed. Five of them will be served in the restaurant today and three tomorrow. These last three dishes take a long time to prepare and so must be assembled a day ahead. Everything else will be assembled as close as possible to the time of cooking. There are no surprises on André's list. In fact, five of these dishes are listed on the "to do" list Bill made for himself yesterday afternoon, before leaving for home. "I rely on the list," says Bill, as he scans it. "If I don't write something down I tend to forget it."

Bill's list consists of twenty items. His is so much longer than André's because André concerns himself primarily with the specials and with parties, leaving the responsibility of tracking the inventory and preparation of standard menu items and desserts to Bill. He also relies on Bill to handle any days-in-advance preparation of ingredients that will be required for the week's specials. These specials are planned by André and posted in the kitchen for everyone to see at the end of the previous week.

In keeping with this responsibility, Bill made a notation on his list to "smoke muscovy." Smoked breast of muscovy duck is the lunch special two days from now. It needs to be smoked in advance so that its smoked flavor will mellow.

Bill knew that André wanted to serve the duck with pears, and so he wrote "pears" on his list. Their vegetable purveyor, who also supplies them with some fruit, was not able to find ripe pears, and so, on his way to work this morning, Bill walked around the corner to see how the pears looked at the Korean market. They were rock hard. Knowing they wouldn't ripen in two days, Bill will tell André they need to go with his second-choice side dish—figs.

When deciding how much to make of the specials, Bill generally halves the number of confirmed reservations. Since there are sixty reservations for lunch, enough specials to feed thirty will be made.

Next, Bill opens the chef's book, a black-and-white hardcover composition notebook, the kind we all used in grammar school, and checks on what meat and fish André ordered yesterday. Every night, after the restaurant is closed, André walks through the downstairs refrigerator, seeing how much meat and fish were used and what needs to be replenished. He writes down what's missing in this notebook, then leaves his orders on his suppliers' answering machines. After placing each order, André runs a pencil line through its listing in the notebook. If it isn't crossed out, that's a signal to Bill that the order was not placed—generally because the supplier's answering machine wasn't connected or the message tape was full—and that Bill should place the order in the morning. But today a penciled line runs through each order.

Putting the notebook back on the shelf, Bill looks inside the refrigerators and freezers to see how much of their already prepared inventory, such as the salmon *en croûte* and the frozen raspberry soufflé, was used up at last night's dinner. He sees more stuffed artichokes than expected. He'd thought they would be gone and that Joe would have to make some today. With an air of satisfaction he crosses "artichokes" off his list and says, "I look forward to crossing things off here."

His inventory check complete, Bill now starts on his prep work. He selects the *arlequin,* or multicolored, vegetable terrine—a dish that appeared on both his list and André's—as his first task because it must be ready for today's lunch and needs to bake three hours. He preheats the combi oven and takes three purees, tomato, spinach, and cheese, out of the refrigerator. Knowing that he would be cooking the terrine today, he made these purees yesterday. He pours the tomato puree into two terrine pans and puts them into the combi oven. This first layer must bake until it is firm so that the next, different-colored, layer won't mix with it.

Once the tomato layer is ready, Bill will pour in the Swiss cheese puree, bake that, and follow up with the spinach puree, and the two terrines will be finished.

As Bill closes the oven door, Joe arrives, calls hello to Bill, and changes into his work clothes in the alcove where the lockers are. Very tall and fresh-faced, he towers over Bill and despite his age has the air of an adolescent who has not yet fully grown into his body. As serious as Bill—when it comes to work, anyway—Joe scans André's list and then Bill's. Like Bill, he uses these lists as road maps to his day's activities.

Joe, who started working here in January 1990, does whatever Bill asks him to do and also has responsibilities that are all his own. He is the one who smokes and marinates the salmon; makes all the ice creams, sorbets, noodles, and spaetzle; prepares the julienned vegetables and artichokes; and makes the garnishes for the lunch specials.

Seeing that many of his responsibilities are on Bill's list, he starts filling them according to priorities he sets for himself. He begins with the spaetzle, since the stove in the small outer room is free and he figures he'll take it while he can get it. After whisking eggs and stirring in flour, salt, nutmeg, and water, he shapes the spaetzle by placing a colander over the pot of boiling water and pushing the batter through the colander's holes.

When this job is done, Joe remains in the outer room to make the day's supply of vanilla ice cream. He chooses this as his second task because it too involves using the little stove. Working methodically, efficiently, he heats milk with two pods of vanilla. (Another example of how nothing is wasted: this vanilla will be used three more times on later days—once whole in another day's batch of ice cream, then just the vanilla beans for some more ice cream, and then the beans again to make granulated vanilla sugar for baking.) In a mixing bowl Joe whisks egg yolks, adds sugar, and then slowly whisks the hot milk into the egg-yolk mixture. Having removed the vanilla, he puts the whole concoction back on the flame, where he watches it carefully. If he overcooks it, he will have scrambled eggs; if he undercooks it, the mixture will be a sauce and not ice cream.

When it's just thick enough, he takes the pot off the flame and pours the liquid through a sieve into an empty container he's positioned in a tub of ice. The sieve takes out any lumps and the ice quickly cools the milk. He then adds one quart of heavy cream and pours the mixture into the ice-cream maker across from the oven.

He sets a timer for seven minutes and goes on to his next priority, which is the marinated salmon because the longer it marinates, the better the flavor will be.

For this dish, a whole salmon was cleaned and deboned yesterday. Joe salted it and left it in the refrigerator for seven hours; it is the salt that "cooks" the fish. Since his workday would be over by the time the fish was ready, he left a note for the dinner kitchen staff, telling them when the seven hours would be up. Someone from the dinner staff took the salmon from the refrigerator, rinsed it, and let it soak for half an hour to get the rest of the salt out. Then he wrapped it in a white towel and put it back into the refrigerator.

Joe now makes a bed of fresh dill stems on the bottom of a long narrow metal tray, unwraps the salmon, and places it on the dill. He sprinkles the salmon with coarse black pepper and then finely chops some dill leaves, mixes them with a little olive oil to make a paste, and pats this paste on top of the fish. He covers the fish with plastic wrap and places it back in the refrigerator, where it will happily soak up the oil-and-dill marinade. The whole fish will remain here, and when the waiters get an order for salmon, they will come down to the kitchen and cut thin slices of it, scraping off the dill.

The timer goes off. Joe retrieves the ice cream and puts it in one of the freezers. Carrying three whole cleaned, salted salmon that have air-dried overnight in the refrigerator, he goes back into the little room and places the fish in the smoker, where hot charcoal and a pinch each of apple wood (which André brings back from the woods behind his country house) and dried apple peelings will smoke the salmon for forty minutes.

Back in the main room, as Bill rolls his eyes, Joe takes a pen out of Bill's shirt pocket and uses it to cross the dishes he's completed off Bill's list. "He always has to use my pen," says Bill, shaking his head in mock annoyance. "And I bought him all those." He points to a few pens that lie scattered on the shelf that stretches the length of his workstation.

"Yeah, but I like *this* one," says Joe, grinning as he sticks the pen back in Bill's pocket. As they methodically press on with their work—Bill is making an appetizer special, pastry stuffed with crab and scallops, which will be offered at both lunch and dinner—they banter back and forth, talking about what happened last night at the cooking class Bill teaches in New Jersey.

Although Joe is only twenty-four, he already has ten years of kitchen experience under his belt. He took his first kitchen job—washing pots and pans—when he was fourteen. "My principal had to sign papers that I was allowed to work that young," he says. "I took that job for money but I always cooked in my house with my family. I always liked it."

Rather than go to cooking school, he apprenticed for two years at L'Hostellerie Bressane in Hillsdale, New York, whose chef, John Morel, is known for training excellent young cooks. Morel, who has known André for thirty years, says he thinks Lutèce is the best restaurant in the city. "I've been there many times," he says. "I judge it as a professional, and André certainly achieves the best food. He is able to produce a lot of different dishes that taste the way they should taste. Like when you make fillet of sole stuffed with tomato, you want it to taste like fillet of sole and not tomato. André does that with everything.

"As for André personally, he is a man who is honest with what he is doing. He is not overcharging. He uses the best quality available and has as many employees as needed to produce what he produces. I also respect a man who works ten or twelve hours a day."

When Morel, who had already placed two apprentices with

Lutèce, heard André had an opening in his kitchen in 1990, he quickly recommended Joe. He's the kind of guy older adults call a good kid—his earnest and helpful nature is immediately apparent.

Slightly before seven, just as Joe crosses another item off the list, Ramon Nunez and Bernardo Rodriguez arrive for work. These two Spanish-speaking men are the ones who clean the raw ingredients and make some basic preparations. The shy Bernardo says a quiet hello and the gruff Ramon grunts and nods as both Bill and Joe grin. Their grins signify that now the fun will begin.

Bill and Ramon, who has worked here for twenty-five years, constantly give each other a hard time. "It's like cat and mouse all day," says Bill. "He's a big buster. He'll say he needs the counter where you are and then when you give it to him he'll say he needs the counter where you've moved to."

Ramon gives me his point of view, but he speaks English with such a heavy accent and so quickly that it is hard for me to understand him, and Bill has to translate: "We fight like cat and dog," Ramon says and Bill repeats this to me. "But now I go to church so everyone is my brother." I laugh but Ramon nods solemnly and says he is quite serious. It seems that if he hadn't started going to church he might still dislike Bill.

"And now you're brothers," I say. Ramon nods.

"It *is* like a family," says Bill. "There's no turnover here, so you really get to know people and we're more relaxed here than they are at other restaurants. You can't walk by someone without saying something. It's like at home I wouldn't walk by my wife without saying something. Joe's come to my house for parties. We go out. For my son's christening, Henry [the *sous-chef* who prepares the fish dishes, and whom we'll meet later] came over and helped me set up."

As we talk Ramon gets out the utensils he'll need for the day's work. He's responsible for peeling the asparagus, making the petits fours and cookies, cleaning the fish and breaking it down into assorted cuts, and wrapping beef or fish in pastry. He also makes the basic fish mousseline.

Bernardo, who is responsible for placing the restaurant's daily laundry order, arrived carrying a few clean white jackets and a pile of white hand towels. Clean linen for the restaurant is delivered every morning around six-thirty and is left outside the door to the basement of an apartment house located a few buildings west on Fiftieth Street. Lutèce rents four rooms in this basement to use as a wine cellar, storage space, and dressing area for Ramon, Bernardo, and the dining-room staff.

After he puts the clean laundry away Bernardo starts washing heads of lettuce, leaf by leaf. The small, brown-haired, brown-eyed, gentle man has worked here for six years. He is responsible for cleaning all of the poultry—chickens, ducks, and pheasants—as well as some vegetables, and for making the mayonnaise and preparing the escargot. Besides this he pitches in wherever Bill or Joe need him to.

The men who work down here will have minimal contact with many of the other employees at Lutèce. Just as a meal is composed of different courses, a restaurant is composed of different groups, most of which are defined by their location within the building: prep kitchen, hot kitchen, bar, dining room, office, coat-check room, cash register area. Although the boundaries of these self-contained units are sometimes crossed—when a waiter's arm reaches into the upstairs kitchen for a dish or when a cook, wondering what quantities to prepare, leafs through the reservations book—and although each unit relies on the others—the waiters know the kitchen will cook well, the kitchen knows the captains will sell what they've prepared—an employee's experience of the restaurant is almost completely centered on what happens within his own work space.

★   ★   ★   ★

Outside the restaurant there is a world that is equally important to the proper preparation and presentation of good food—the world of the meat, fish, and vegetable suppliers.

For years a myth has been propagated by American restaurateurs that all chefs worth their toques begin the day in the wee hours by going to the meat or fish or vegetable markets, personally picking the freshest products available, and having them shipped back to their restaurants.

That myth "sounds good but is just a lot of blah blah blah," André told me. "You can't go to the market and cook. You'd be up at three in the morning and cooking until midnight. You'd sleep for only three hours.

"In France everyone goes to the market," he continues. "But what you do is walk around to your different suppliers and give them a list of what you need and they get it together for you. Meanwhile you sit down and have a glass of Beaujolais with your friends while the suppliers pick out the food and put it in your car."

Even if it was physically possible, he says, "it would be pointless for me to go to market. I would be a small purchaser and so would not get the first choice of the best merchandise. But my suppliers are important purchasers and I am important to them, so I get the best of the best. I've worked with many of my suppliers for over twenty years. They know what I want and they know that if I do not have the best quality and the freshest merchandise, then I will not accept it."

Each of these companies sends a representative to Lutèce every morning. Crossing the threshold of the cellar door and entering the prep kitchen, these individuals deliver the raw ingredients that are so important to the cooks. To us what they carry may be just meat or fish or vegetables. But every carton represents another story, another company, another dream.

ℬass en croûte

FOR 12 PEOPLE

1 4-lb. bass (ask fish
  store to split bass
  lengthwise and
  remove the bones and
  skin)
Parsley
Tarragon

2 lbs. mousseline of pike
  (recipe below)
2 lbs. puff pastry (Lutèce
  makes its own, but
  you can use frozen)
Sauce choron (recipe
  follows)

Poach bass in boiling water for 15 seconds. Remove and place on a dry cloth. On half of the bass, place parsley, chopped tarragon, and the mousseline. Top with other half of bass.

Roll out puff pastry, the same length as the fish, and cut into 2 equal parts. Place the whole bass on one half, then cover up with the other. With fingers, close pastry all around in the shape of the fish. You can imitate scales by using the metal nozzle of a pastry bag.

Cook in medium oven (350 degrees) for 40 minutes. Serve hot accompanied by the *sauce choron*. You can also let cool and serve with a mayonnaise.

MOUSSELINE

1 lb. pike fillet
3 eggs
1 tsp salt

Pepper to taste
2 cups chilled heavy
  cream

Process pike in food processor for 30 seconds until it resembles a paste. Add eggs, salt, and pepper, and process for another 30 seconds. Stir in the cream. It must be cold; otherwise the mixture will separate.

$\mathcal{S}$AUCE CHORON

SAUCE BÉARNAISE FLAVORED WITH TOMATO

YIELD: 1½ CUPS

2 Tb tarragon vinegar
2 Tb dry white wine
1 Tb chopped shallots
1½ Tb chopped fresh
   tarragon (or tarragon
   preserved in vinegar)
1½ Tb chopped fresh
   chervil
1 pinch salt
1 pinch freshly ground
   pepper

3 egg yolks
1 tsp water
12 Tb unsalted butter
   (1½ sticks)
1 scant tsp lemon juice
2 Tb tomato pulp,
   chopped fine, cooked
   in a saucepan for 1
   to 2 minutes, and
   drained

Place the vinegar and wine in a stainless steel or enameled saucepan. Add the chopped shallots, ½ tablespoon of the tarragon, ½ tablespoon of the chervil, salt, and pepper. Over high heat, reduce by ⅔ and allow to cool to lukewarm.

Beat in the egg yolks and 1 teaspoon of water. With the saucepan on the edge of a low flame (or in a pan of warm water), whisk the sauce constantly until it begins to thicken.

When the sauce has begun to thicken, beat in the butter, a small piece at a time, whisking in one piece completely before adding the next.

When the butter is completely incorporated, add lemon juice. Strain the sauce through a fine sieve. Stir in the remaining tarragon and chervil.

Stir in the tomato.

This sauce cannot be refrigerated and reused, but it can be kept warm, in a bain-marie of warm water, in a warm place, for an hour or two.

7:00 A.M.

*L*utèce has two main suppliers for meat (the larger is DeBragga and Spitler), two for fish (primarily Rozzo and Sons), one for game and poultry (D'Artagnan), and one (Dom's Market) for basic vegetables: asparagus, onions, carrots, celery, and potatoes. Besides these companies it uses about twenty smaller ones for specialty items. For example, its lobsters come from a company called New York Fish House; mesclun salad from Four Winds; various mushrooms from Aux Delices des Bois; tomatoes from Sunrise Sun-Ripened Tomatoes; bread from Tom Cat Bakery, and Swiss coffee from La Semeuse. In addition, it calls upon more than a few far-flung companies, like Fresh and Wild in Oregon, which will ship morels, cepes, or chanterelles UPS when they are in season and throw in some huckleberries while they're at it, or Sea Farm in the state of Washington, which will ship sturgeon by overnight UPS delivery.

Also, on summer Sundays André will stop at farms in upstate New York to buy some fruits and vegetables. Although he can't handpick all his products, he expects his suppliers to send him only produce that is as good as what he would select himself. And if they don't? "I go nuts," says André. "I'm a nice guy but when it comes to that I go crazy because I think he tries to fool me. I am very difficult then. I go out of my mind. Out of control, really. They know that, so in general they are very careful."

Because of André's temper, Marc Sarrazin—one of André's best friends and the head of DeBragga and Spitler—hasn't worked directly with him in years but lets another partner handle his account. André confirms this, saying, "Sometimes it's difficult to deal with friends. If something is not right, I tell him and he sends me to hell and I send him to hell. It's easier to deal with someone else because, with Marc, I am like a brother."

"If André wants salmon," says Phil Rozzo, president of Rozzo and Sons, "we'll go through four, maybe five, boxes of fish until we find two fish for him. He wants them so fresh that they're swimming down Fiftieth Street." And if they're not? Rozzo shakes his head and says, "His temper. You gotta watch out for that temper. It's better now than in the old days but still . . ." He shakes his head again.

In exchange for the preferential treatment his suppliers give him, André remains not only a quick-paying customer but a loyal one. He's worked with Rozzo since the day Lutèce opened and with Sarrazin for almost as long. I witnessed him turn away many suppliers soliciting his business, saying he was very happy with his current suppliers, thank you very much.

He's been with the same vegetable supplier, Dom's Market, for five years, ever since his previous vegetable supplier went out of business. Five years is a short time for André, but the fact that he's used the same supplier for even that long elicited astonishment from Matthew D'Arrigo, vice president of D'Arrigo Brothers, one of the wholesalers from which Dom's Market purchases vegetables for Lutèce.

"Five years is very loyal," D'Arrigo says. "You usually don't find restaurants doing that. They get in a snit, and boom, out the door, let's go to the next guy. Five years is rare. Chefs always end up worrying about whether they're getting charged too much. They always want to know, 'Why is the product no good? And why, if it's no good, is it so expensive at the same time?'

"That's just the way the produce business works," D'Arrigo says. "When it's short, it's high-priced, and also it's short for a reason— the quality is bad. With bumper crops, beautiful crops, you'll see cheap prices. It's the reverse of what you'd think would be true. You'd think if the stuff is beautiful you'd have to pay more for it, but no, it means it's probably oversupplied and you can have it cheap."

André understands all that, says Jack Gargiulo, owner of Dom's Market. He was referred to André by Barry Wine, chef/owner of the Quilted Giraffe, which was one of New York City's other four-star restaurants until it closed in December 1992.

"I like the relationship because he appreciates his suppliers," says Gargiulo. "It becomes a marriage. There's no price quotations, no nonsense, no sending back things because he thinks they might not last. He knows what he needs and that's what he orders. And he only demands what's reasonable. If there are variables involved that don't allow us to get a good product, he'd just as soon do without it. His philosophy is similar to the philosophy of The Four Seasons. If it's not good, he'll pass. It's not something where I'd have to provide garbage."

Would any restaurant want "garbage"? Believe it or not, the answer is yes. These are the customers Gargiulo refers to as "quotation" customers. These restaurants ask their suppliers to give them daily price quotations, and the restaurants then lock in to the best price from one of many suppliers. Lutèce never does this.

"Lutèce is owner-operated," says Gargiulo. "He's there. He sees the merchandise. He realizes that someone who is legitimate, who is in business a long time, is not out to hurt him."

But, Gargiulo continues, "if I were to open a restaurant and I wasn't there and I had somebody else running it, I would definitely want competitive pricing. This way I would know that my chef isn't on the take and my purchasing agent isn't on the take and the dealer isn't giving me the runaround."

The downside of price quotations, says Gargiulo, is that "there's no way to give them a better product. Absentee owners look purely and simply at a number on a piece of paper. Restaurants that are down to number-crunching are no longer concerned about staying in the very best of quality. They're concerned about staying in the very best of price. Now you create a compromise. He can no longer say, 'Give me the best berry you have,' or 'Give me the best melon you have.' He's going to say, 'How much?' He'll take the cheaper one, and so whoever goes to eat there is going to get a decent melon but they aren't going to get the best.

"There are certain varieties of strawberries that are wonderful tasting, tender, and have a nice appearance. They do not have a tremendous shelf life but at least they'll taste like a strawberry. Then there [are other strawberries] which are like stones. They'll last forever and they're pretty as anything but they're fairly hollow inside and they're very tart and not good to eat. This is what the quotation customers will take over the better berries. They're so afraid that by Monday they're going to lose three pints out of a flat that they'll take the strongest, heartiest package there is, regardless of quality or taste."

Today's first delivery arrives at 7:10 from Dom's Market, each item packaged separately, in its own wooden box or paper carton. Although most of these vegetables and fruits have traveled thousands of miles to get here, they look fresh-picked and each has a story to tell. As Jack Gargiulo says, "A bunch of leeks is not just a bunch of leeks. It's California, with long white stems. It's local, with long green. It's local, with maybe dirt from the last rain. It's from Guatemala . . . fresh and beautiful. And that's just leeks."

All of the produce, especially if it is imported, has gone through at least half a dozen different hands before arriving here: from the grower, to the packer, to the shipper, then onto a train, a truck, or a plane. If it comes from a foreign country, it must pass inspection by the Food and Drug Administration, usually at the point of shipping. If a bug is found, the produce is usually fumigated, and if the levels of pesticide are too high, the produce is destroyed.

Once they pass inspection, the foreign vegetables and fruits are flown into this country, where they are picked up at the airport by an importer, who then resells them to wholesalers. He loads the goods onto another plane, or more often a truck, and delivers them to his clients.

Today's delivery to Lutèce comprises leeks from California, asparagus and raspberries from Chile, Boston lettuce and carrots from California, Yukon Gold potatoes from Washington State, string beans from Guatemala, and onions from Colorado. In different months the fruits and vegetables will have different points of origin. Asparagus, for example, once limited to a ten-week California growing season, is now available year-round, thanks to a broadened base of supply. The California season starts in March around St. Patrick's Day and ends by the first week in June. Halfway through the California growing season, the Washington season begins, and it runs into late August, at which point Mexico picks up the slack for one month. In late September Chile starts shipping. In October Peru ships alongside Chile. Chile finishes in December, at which point asparagus becomes the bailiwick of Peru. In late January Mexico begins shipping again and, after that, in March, it's back to California. Local eastern asparagus is not sold to restaurants because it cannot compete in terms of quality.

"Asparagus is *the* vegetable with rich-people appeal. It's number one by far. There's nothing even close," says D'Arrigo, whose company is the largest asparagus distributor at the Hunts Point Market. "If there's no asparagus, people are going crazy for it. Dom's Market will buy asparagus at any price . . . because he has to get it to Lutèce. It's one of those high-ticket dinner-plate items in Manhattan restaurants."

High-ticket indeed. Asparagus is expensive because it must be picked and packed by hand. As is true of all vegetables, its price swings are determined by supply and demand—the less asparagus available, the higher the price will be. But unlike other vegetables, whose price plummets when there is an abundant supply, asparagus is always pricey. Green peppers, for instance, can go as low as ten cents a pound, whereas the minimum wholesale cost for asparagus rarely goes below one dollar a pound and can go as high as four dollars a pound.

Asparagus (whose name comes from the Greek *spargan,* "to swell") is a perennial plant of the lily family. It is raised from seed in a nursery, and farmers then take the seedlings and transplant them into their fields. Like flower bulbs, the seedlings are planted under the ground and after about eighteen months they start producing a crop that can be harvested. The edible young shoots are white when they come out of the ground and turn green with exposure to sunlight. Once these spears approach a length of eight inches they are cut by hand.

Hand cutting—a labor-intensive operation, to say the least—is necessary because an individual plant produces spears over a period of time, so that some spears may be only two inches long while others are six or eight inches. (The diameter of the spears is determined by how close to each other the seedlings are planted —the closer together, the smaller the spears.)

"It's the ugliest crop," says D'Arrigo. "You look at a field of dirt and the farmers tell you, 'That's asparagus,' and you go, 'Well, when are you going to plant it? Where is it?' and in two weeks' time it'll just be . . . whoosh . . . flying up. It's a weed. It grows very fast.

"It's turned on and off by irrigation," he continues. "If you water asparagus, it will grow. If you stop watering it, it will stop growing. [Farmers] can manipulate their fields that way. You can have a field of asparagus and divide it in half and water just one side of it and produce a crop and the other half will stay dormant."

After the harvest, small farmers sell their crop to a packing-and-shipping company, which handsorts the asparagus by size and handpacks them. In the end, asparagus grown by many farmers will be sold under the same label.

Since the levels of chemicals and pesticides American farmers can use are strictly controlled by the federal government, domestic vegetables do not need to be inspected after the harvest. Because the produce wholesalers do not process or in any way change the content of any fruits or vegetables, their facilities and working methods are also not inspected. However, in order to ensure uniformity of quality and price, the United States Department of Agriculture (USDA), at the produce industry's request, instituted certain grade standards, to which the industry adheres. In the case of asparagus, a top grade of USDA #1 signifies fresh dark green stalks whose tips are well formed, tight, and free of field dirt and sand.

If a wholesaler feels that the product he has been shipped does not meet USDA #1 standards but his shipper feels that it does, the burden of proof falls on the wholesaler. He can call in a USDA inspector and pay the agency a fee to have the product officially graded. The USDA's decision is final.

All produce is sold under a brand name, and buyers know that some labels (for instance, Lee Brands and Andy Boy, for asparagus) tend to represent a consistently higher quality than others. But even quality labels can be off, thanks to poor weather, or a truck that loses its refrigeration, or a foreman who leaves the shipment outdoors in twenty-degree weather, or an airline that loses the shipment for three days.

Knowing this, Dom's Market will never simply buy a brand name. Before committing himself to buy, Gargiulo will ask the seller, "How are they [the asparagus] running?" If they are not "running" well at one supplier's, Gargiulo will call a second and a third until he finds asparagus of better quality. And if he doesn't, he'll call André and say it just isn't available. This rarely happens with asparagus since Gargiulo protects himself from running up against shortages or low quality by having asparagus shipped to him directly from Chile during September, October, and November, a time of year when a shortage is most likely.

Lutèce always buys jumbo asparagus because André believes they are the most tender and flavorful. The asparagus that arrived at Lutèce this morning came into Jack's Manhattan facility yesterday from the Hunts Point Market in the Bronx. "Before Jacques orders [at three in the afternoon each day], I already have one hundred boxes of asparagus on the way in," says Gargiulo. Just as Lutèce must anticipate the needs of its patrons and order the day before, so too must Gargiulo anticipate the needs of *his* clients. If he runs short of something he can always cover the demand for it by buying through his broker at Hunts Point. These vegetables would arrive at Dom's at around five in the morning, in time to be loaded onto Dom's delivery trucks, which leave the premises every morning at around seven. Dom's is open twenty-four hours a day during the week. It is closed only from Saturday noon through Sunday evening at six.

The vegetables kept in inventory at Dom's are those with a shelf life of more than a few days: carrots, broccoli, cauliflower, potatoes, and asparagus. From the time it's harvested, asparagus, if kept at thirty-seven degrees, can survive for two weeks without any noticeable change in quality. On the other hand, mushrooms, raspberries, and most lettuces need to be ordered daily.

With a customer base of 250 steady mid- to high-end restaurants and hotels, including Lutèce, The Four Seasons, La Côte Basque, La Grenouille, and The Plaza, Dom's knows it needs a certain minimum of each vegetable. Daily it will send out approximately twelve hundred pounds of asparagus, four thousand pounds of carrots, two hundred pounds of string beans, and five thousand pounds of onions.

To ensure a steady supply at times of scarcity, Gargiulo also buys strawberries, raspberries, celery root, asparagus, and shallots directly from their growers. To fill in any gaps in this supply, and also when these products are available in abundance, he will buy from the terminal markets at Hunts Point and in Philadelphia.

Terminal markets are last stops for trains and trucks carrying considerable loads of merchandise. The Hunts Point Market in the Bronx, where Gargiulo does most of his buying, used to be in lower Manhattan, where it was established in the seventeenth century. It was called Washington Market and extended from the site of today's World Trade Center on the south to Canal Street on the north, east as far as Greenwich Street and west to the river.

The market was on city-owned land, and "the City of New York decided that the land was more valuable for places like the World Trade Center," says Ira Cohen, whose firm, Shapiro and Cohen, has headquarters at Hunts Point, and who sits on the market's board of directors. "They couldn't just shovel us off into the Hudson River since we generate a lot of money, tax revenue, and jobs. And so in 1967 the city built this one-hundred-thirteen-acre facility on what was once a swamp in the Bronx."

The merchants relocated and in time decided that they could run the market better than the city did. They bought the market from the city in 1986, and the sixty-seven merchants now pay a ground lease to the city and own and operate the market themselves.

The South Bronx is better known for its high crime rate than for high-quality produce. But in one corner of it these fruit and vegetable purveyors do a bustling business behind a fenced-in fortress, complete with armed guards and security gates through which all vehicular and foot traffic must pass. Eighteen-wheelers roar in one after another, and several times a day a train comes through, delivering produce from thirty-five countries and forty-nine states.

Policies in the market are set by the board of directors, and, like a small city, the market is responsible for its own security, sanitation, and maintenance. The area is divided by four streets, each half a mile long, flanked by two-story bright blue buildings. These buildings hold individual warehouses standing side by side on the first floors and individual offices on the second.

The arriving merchandise is unloaded from the trucks and trains behind each warehouse. I had expected to see trucks, but the trains were surprising. "The trains are part of the romance of the industry," says Myra Gordon, who is executive administrative director of the market and is one of the few females among the ten thousand employees. "You can sit upstairs in the office and about six o'clock at night the train man comes through and he rings the bell and he stops and waves."

The trains bring in only what Gordon calls "the hardware of the industry"—foods, such as broccoli, carrots, potatoes, and onions, that have a long shelf life. Although a rail car can carry twice as much as a truck and is cheaper, many wholesalers don't use the trains because it takes them longer to get here. A truck from California arrives in New York within five days, whereas a train takes ten.

Two rows of rails run behind every warehouse in the market. At the time allotted to each row of warehouses, the train comes through and drops off full railcars in front of the appropriate warehouses. When the cars are empty, the train engine returns and picks them up.

Inside each warehouse, the produce is stacked on open metal racks that stand twenty-nine feet high, reaching all the way to the ceiling. Once it's sold, the merchandise is sent out via handcarts or forklifts, whose operators drive them through huge garage-style front doors, pushing aside the long vertical plastic tabs that are there to keep out the outside heat or cold. Frequently honking to get people out of their way, the forklift operators drive up to the backs of the waiting trucks, into which the merchandise is then loaded.

Dom's Market will start its daily buying at eight each night. At that time, the broker who works for Dom's, as well as for a few other companies, arrives at Hunts Point and begins to assess the worldwide market by calling various growers, as well as the wholesalers (the market is too big for him to visit each wholesaler in person). Although he buys the few vegetables Dom's may not have in stock each night, the broker's primary function is to feed Gargiulo information.

Being a broker at Hunts Point is similar to being a broker on Wall Street—every piece of information passed along to clients will affect how the clients will buy today and tomorrow. Produce prices are determined by supply and demand, and they can change in a few hours simply because of information on crop abundance or scarcity, flood or cold warnings, a train derailment, a plane crash, or a massive fumigation. It is not unusual for prices to triple in five minutes because of news of a freeze at a grower's location. Since weather is the most significant factor in the condition and price of produce, the broker's conversations with growers and wholesalers center on weather conditions at the point of shipping.

If a broker hears any rumblings of trouble, he will immediately buy all the affected merchandise he can for his clients. On the other hand, if there are no problems and a crop is plentiful, he will wait, in the belief that the produce will be available cheaper later in the night. Since produce deteriorates with every passing minute, the vendors will indeed drop their prices with every passing hour.

Gargiulo leaves for work at two-thirty in the morning. "The minute I get in the car I call in to my broker," he says. "He gives me a rundown of market conditions. I know, from the day before, what looks good and what doesn't look good pricewise. I tell him right as we speak to lock up certain lots of merchandise. After I speak with him I talk to my broker in Philadelphia and tell him to lock into all the lots of merchandise I can not get at good prices or good quality in this market. As soon as I get to the office I start working on my own, trying to augment my supply with various contacts I have in the market. I spend a solid five hours every day doing the buying."

Over the years Gargiulo, who started working in this family business when he was thirteen and has been head of the company since 1972, has earned himself a reputation as a shrewd buyer.

"Jack is probably one of the best buyers in the industry," says the wholesaler Matthew D'Arrigo. "He's what we call a barometer. I usually get better money than Jack wants to pay. When he calls me, I know asparagus is scarce. He's probably on his fourth call. He's desperate."

"Buying," says Gargiulo, "is not just product or point-of-origin information. It's the inflection in the person's voice. It's the time of day they call. It's the sequence they offer me the item in. I'm a people studier. I can tell, just by how they ask, how much I can get out of them. It's a give-and-take. Like a prize fight. You let someone hit you light twice, then you hit them hard."

The order that arrived at Lutèce at ten minutes after seven was loaded onto the back of one of Dom's refrigerated trucks at around one in the morning. The order, but for a carton of snow peas, was filled from Dom's inventory at the warehouse. The snow peas were purchased by the broker at Hunts Point during the night. As it does every night, Dom's sent a truck to the Bronx at around nine to load the merchandise needed to fill the gaps in today's orders. This truck loads until three-thirty in the morning and then returns to Dom's.

"We have twelve or fourteen trucks just waiting for this merchandise, and it flies out of here," says Gargiulo. The bulk of Dom's orders from Hunts Point, as well as a trailer from Philadelphia, will arrive later in the day. This will be stored in the refrigerated warehouse area until all the orders from the various restaurants for the following day are in. These orders are then filled and loaded onto the trucks. Whatever is not in stock will again be purchased by the broker at Hunts Point and driven down to Dom's.

Once the vegetables reach Lutèce, Bill or Joe inspect their quality and size, and if all is copacetic, they sign the purchase order, keep one copy, hand the other back to Dom's driver. The asparagus is given to Ramon, who starts peeling them. The rest of the vegetables are put in the refrigerator, behind the ones that are already there. The "first in/first out" rule is strictly adhered to for all perishables.

★ ★ ★ ★

Another delivery man soon walks in carrying a large gray plastic box from DeBragga and Spitler filled with one strip of beef (from which the steaks will be cut), one beef fillet (for filet mignon), five racks of lamb, two loins of veal, and five pounds of jumbo calf sweetbreads. The latter are perhaps the most mysterious items served in French restaurants. Many customers love them but have no idea what they are; others think they are anything from brains to intestinal organs. They are, in fact, the thymus glands of calves.

Bill checks the meat for freshness, weighs it, piece by piece, on a large scale, and then places it on the counter to the right of the kitchen's exit, where it will await the noon arrival of the young cook responsible for dressing it. This room is air-conditioned to help products retain their freshness and to keep pastry dough from sticking. In the winter it is not heated and it often gets so cold that Bill sometimes wears three pairs of socks. Working here is like working in a refrigerator, and that's why the meat can be left out for so long.

Behind the meat that just arrived lies the story of André's friendship with Marc Sarrazin, which began in 1962. (Sarrazin has passed the title of president on to his son, Marc Sarrazin, Jr., but has remained active in the company.)

While the general public wouldn't recognize his name, Sarrazin is as well known within the restaurant world as André. In 1987 *The New York Times* profiled Sarrazin, calling him "the best-connected, most influential man" in the restaurant business.

"Over the years," the newspaper wrote, "he has become a vital communications link, mostly on the East Coast, between chefs and restaurateurs seeking staff members, and cooks seeking work in the United States and France. His connections have resulted in the placement of hundreds of cooks and chefs in scores of restaurants."

Although André takes an obvious delight in Sarrazin, seeing him once a week and talking to him on the telephone almost every day ("Our wives think we are washwomen, the way we talk on the phone," says Sarrazin), I must admit that meeting Lutèce's "meat man" was the least promising part of this project to me. I don't know about you, but I've never really wanted to think about the fact that the beef on my plate was once a cow or that the chicken roasting in the oven once had a head and legs and a mother who loved it.

I've always felt sorry for butchers. What sad twist of fate led them to this gross job? I'd think as I watched the men in blood-spattered white coats behind the counter at the local butcher shop hacking and grinding their way through an honest day's work.

Imagine my surprise when Sarrazin proudly told me: "I am a

butcher. I do not know anything else, except being a butcher, and I knew I wanted to be one from the time I was four years old."

He *wanted* to be a butcher? Why? "Don't ask me why," he said in his very heavily accented English. "Maybe it was because we lived next door to a slaughterhouse. My whole life has been the meat industry. I slaughtered my first animal when I was nine years old. I held the knife and the butcher held my hand and I killed a lamb."

Sarrazin, who grew up in the tiny French town of Charolles, left school when he was fourteen to apprentice as a butcher. He then did everything on the meat circuit, from working in a slaughterhouse to livestock buying to working in a retail store. He came to this country in 1953 and the following year landed a job as salesman with DeBragga and Spitler. He bought the company in 1973. Today there are three partners besides the Sarrazins—two who handle the ordering and buying and oversee the butchers, and another who handles sales. The two Sarrazins handle the PR and marketing.

A few days before my 6:00 A.M. visit to the company, I mentioned to Bill at Lutèce that I was going to watch how their meat orders are processed. "Wear old clothes," he said. "The blood is going to be flying."

That's what I thought too, and given my lack of appreciation for blood, as well as my aversion to getting up early enough to be *anywhere* at six, I was less than enthusiastic about my visit. I expected to see huge trucks unloading dead animals, but this was not the case. Although lots of small trucks and vans were double-parked in front of the various warehouses and two large trucks were indeed unloading across the street from DeBragga and Spitler, I didn't see a single carcass. At the time of my arrival, everything coming off the large trucks was in white boxes and everything going into the smaller ones was paper wrapped and placed in large plastic containers.

"The industry has changed a lot in the last fifteen years," the younger Sarrazin told me as he gave me a tour of the company, tucked away in a little annex off Washington Street in the heart of

New York's meat district, an industrial-looking part of Manhattan located west of Eighth Avenue just below Fourteenth Street.

By six, early-morning deliveries to the company had already been completed. Now red-white-and-black DeBragga and Spitler trucks were backed up against the garage-type doors at the front of the building and were being loaded with meat going to hotels, restaurants, and retail shops. Besides Lutèce, names like La Côte Basque, The Rainbow Room, The Plaza, and The Pierre were written on the destination cards placed on top of each large, gray, meat-filled plastic box.

On the whole, the place was significantly less repulsive than I'd imagined. Yes, some veal carcasses were hanging from huge hooks waiting to be sliced into loins or legs, but, probably because their heads were no longer attached, they looked more like huge wads of candle wax than dead animals. The sound of the electric saw cutting through a rib or two was exactly like that of a dentist's drill. Not too bad. And not a drop of blood flew anywhere. As I would come to learn, most of these animals had left their blood elsewhere, namely, at the place of slaughter.

And Marc Sarrazin, Jr., was a nice guy. If I had met him at a party and had to guess his profession, I'd have guessed he was an accountant. He does in fact hold an MBA. Unlike his father, who wanted to be a butcher, Sarrazin junior "tried to do everything but." He was a premed major for a year and a half, "but organic chemistry blew me away." He graduated from college in 1977 with an English degree, "which doesn't prepare you for much." He went to work for his father and attended business school at night to earn his MBA.

"Our market used to be much more lively than it is now," he said, "and some of the glamour is gone." (*Glamour?* I thought.) "There used to be lots of hanging meat." (Whole carcasses are called "hanging" meat because they are shipped hanging on large hooks suspended from rails inside refrigerated trucks. These rails connect with a system of rails that run from outside the meat purveyors' buildings into their refrigerators.)

"With the improvements in vacuum-packaging and modern

technology—better refrigeration, transportation, communication, faxes, wiring money—more and more stuff is being boxed and prepared out West right at the place of slaughter. You don't see that many trailers unloading carcasses anymore."

Although most retail stores and many restaurants are buying meat already butchered and vacuum-packed, some restaurateurs —including André—prefer to have a staff member make the final cuts because, as André says, "it's cheaper to do it yourself." For this reason, DeBragga and Spitler still brings in some hanging veal and lamb. For efficiency's sake, beef is cut and boxed at the slaughterhouse. This eliminates the transport of bone and waste fat, allowing the shippers to fit significantly more meat into each truck.

As they did today, beef, veal, and lamb make up the bulk of André's orders from DeBragga and Spitler. Although all of the beef he gets from this company is Certified Angus Beef (CAB), the best beef available for broad distribution on the American market, André does order some prime non-Angus beef from his other meat supplier, Piccinini Brothers. He uses two suppliers so that he is protected in case one is not able to procure something, and also as a cross-check on price and quality.

CAB comes from Angus cattle, which, to qualify for the CAB label, are graded by the USDA under stricter criteria than other cattle. Although all meat sold in this country that crosses state lines must be inspected, it does not have to be graded. Grading is a voluntary program established in 1927 by the USDA to "facilitate the marketing of beef, making it clear to consumers what they were getting," says Michael L. May, chief of the livestock and meat standardization branch of the livestock and seed division of the agricultural marketing service of the USDA. His division sets the grading standards for meat. The grades, in order of decreasing quality, are prime, choice, and select. CAB comes in both prime and choice grades. The grade is based on marbling (the more marbling, the juicier and more flavorful the meat will be), youth (the younger, the more tender), carcass leanness, fine texture, and firmness.

May's division also helped develop and approve the grading criteria for the CAB marketing program when it was established in 1978. The CAB program was set up to counteract the 1976 lowering of USDA grading standards, which allowed more cattle to qualify for the choice grade. Producers who had invested money in raising high-quality cattle wanted to have their product stand apart from the rest. "The bottom line was that they wanted to get paid what their product was worth," says May.

The CAB program helped consumers too, since it provided them with a guarantee of *consistent* quality, something that the USDA grades no longer did. "You can select beef out of choice or prime grades that's just as good as Certified Angus Beef but Certified Angus is *always* that good. It specifies certain characteristics that have to be at certain levels at all times," says May.

The quality of beef is determined by two things—genetics and what the animals are fed. "Some breeds (particularly Angus cattle) are more likely to produce high-quality beef than others," says May. "But then you have to feed them high-concentrate feed. That means putting them in a feedlot rather than leaving them out on pasture. Very few cattle will make choice or prime grades if they're fed on grass, but if they're on high-concentrate feed they will." Putting the animals on this feed obviously costs the rancher more than just letting them eat grass.

The average life span of cattle being raised for CAB classification is eighteen months. The animals are born after a gestation period of slightly more than nine months. Of the resulting offspring, none will reach sexual maturity—the males will be castrated and the females will not produce a calf. "Castration changes their hormones," says Sarrazin. "They put on weight in a nice way and the castration eliminates the sex drive so they're not so crazy. They don't get themselves all banged and bruised up."

The animals nurse for seven months and are then weaned and sent directly to a feedlot, where they are fed a high-concentrate corn ration until they are ready for slaughter.

At the slaughterhouse the Angus cattle are identified by a CAB employee and stamped with the letter *A*. Like all other meat and poultry that will be sold to businesses, they must be inspected both before and after slaughter.

The killing of the cattle, says Sarrazin, "is not a pretty sight." If it's a kosher slaughter, their throats are slit and bled. Otherwise they're hit with a stun gun in the head, which kills them instantaneously. A chain is wrapped around the hind leg, and the carcass is hoisted up by a machine onto a rail and starts going down the production line. One guy slits the belly and empties the guts, another skins the carcass, etc. After the animal is cut in half lengthwise and any remaining skin and hair scalded off, it is then hung in a refrigerated area for twenty-four hours.

During the entire slaughtering process there are numerous USDA inspectors on the floor, watching all of the steps and checking the health of the organs.

After the carcasses have been hung in the refrigerated chamber, they will either be accepted for the CAB label or rejected, and will be graded either prime or choice. The USDA is so strict with its grading system that it requires meats of different grades to be cut and packaged separately. That means one grade must be cleared completely from the room before another grade can be worked on. This ensures that the grades won't get mixed up or mislabeled. CAB is treated like a separate grade, so that only CAB product is worked on at one time. Non-CAB prime and choice are handled separately.

The CAB is cut into sections and shipped at a temperature of twenty-eight degrees to distributors like DeBragga and Spitler. Trucks bearing this product arrive from the Midwest at the company every Monday or Tuesday. DeBragga and Spitler then ages most of the beef for three to four weeks. Aging causes the muscle fibers to deteriorate, making them tender. André, however, wants his meat aged for no more than fourteen days. "Any longer than that," André says, "and it will get a strong, steakhouse kind of flavor. I don't want that. I just want a little change in taste. And I want it fresh. Sometimes the butchers argue with me. They think I am wrong, but if I had to choose I would choose freshness over a little more tenderness."

The veal served at Lutèce has been fed milk rather than grass. Milk-fed veal is considered the finest quality—tender, pale pink, sweet and delicate in flavor. Grass-fed veal is red and tougher in texture.

Veal, the meat of young calves, is a by-product of the dairy industry. For a dairy cow to produce milk in commercial quantities it must have offspring once a year. Because relatively few of these animals are needed to rebuild the dairy herds, the calves are destined to become veal. They are placed in pens right after birth and kept stationary to prevent the muscles from developing fully. This results in more tender meat.

Unlike beef, which needs to age to develop its full flavor, veal, like pork and organ meats, must be eaten quickly, definitely within a week, or it will spoil. Veal is generally delivered to Lutèce within two days of slaughter.

Lamb, the third meat André ordered for today, is obtained daily by DeBragga and Spitler from a lamb purveyor.

The meat that was just delivered to Lutèce was ordered by André last night after midnight. At 12:30 A.M. one of the partners at DeBragga and Spitler arrived and started taking down all the orders on the answering machine. At 2:00 A.M. he was joined by an employee, who entered the orders into the computer and printed out individual work-order sheets for each account. The partner meanwhile ordered, and accepted deliveries of, provisions the company doesn't keep in stock, such as lamb and sweetbreads. At 4:00 A.M. the partner classified the orders according to geographical routes and arranged them in the order they should be filled.

At 4:30, the foreman for the processing room, where all the meat is cut and wrapped to go out, arrived, pushed the hanging meat out of the refrigerator and into the processing room, and set up the room so that when the butchers arrived at 5:00 A.M. they would be able to get right to work.

Before the butchers could do a thing, however, a USDA inspector had to inspect the entire plant for such things as cleanliness and proper temperatures. If he had found a tiny piece of rust, or the wrong wattage in a light bulb, or a dirty bathroom, the company would have had to rectify its offense before business could proceed.

From the moment the USDA inspector arrives on the site he is allowed to walk through the plant whenever he wants to for the rest of the day. "It's not like they say, 'Okay, we're coming now,' " says Sarrazin. "Boom. They're there looking over your shoulder. We are under continuous federal inspection.

"We have an incredible amount of regulations," he continues. "We have to have a certain temperature of water to steam-clean the iceboxes, the bins. We have to use plastic cutting boards instead of wooden ones. Before the guys go into the bathroom they have to take off their white coats so that the coats don't go into the bathroom with them.

"We get a daily written report from the USDA on where we stand—what has to be done and doesn't have to be done. The USDA keeps us on our toes. We are a very regulated industry, especially as compared to the fish industry." There is no federal inspection of fish, and shellfish is the only seafood inspected by state governments. Seafood purveyors and processing plants also escape federal inspection, although they may be inspected by certain state agencies or town boards of health. On the whole, however, these latter inspections are lax and infrequent.

"Fulton Fish Market in the morning is a pretty interesting sight," Sarrazin continues. "It's not like here, with the guys with white coats and white hats."

★ ★ ★ ★

Ariane Daguin, co-owner of D'Artagnan, the Jersey City–based company that supplies Lutèce with its ducks, game, foie gras, and most of its free-range chickens, also finds the lack of regulation of the fish industry "interesting"—so much so that she will not allow her three-year-old daughter to eat fish.

"Seeing what they do to these fish" has turned Daguin against the product. "I've seen them color shrimp with special stuff to revive their color and I've seen them just drag fish along the floor.

"Everything we make is inspected by the USDA, but if I was to make a fish mousse, I could make it in the sewer for all they would care," she says. Her company is so closely inspected because it processes some food products, like terrines and mousses. But when it comes to products André orders from D'Artagnan, the company doesn't process them in any way. They simply get them in and ship them out.

Daguin seems significantly less tolerant of the USDA inspectors than Sarrazin. She calls the supervisor "a Nazi" and says, "the less we see of him the better." She tells a story of how she once objected when he made her pay an architect to draw up a whole new set of blueprints after she'd added a piece of equipment to her kitchen. She'd thought it would be enough simply to draw the new equipment in on the existing set of blueprints so that she could avoid paying the architect a large fee. But the supervisor said no. "I said, 'You know, you *guys* . . .' and he got so mad that I said 'you guys' to him that now, when he calls, I say, 'Yes, sir, Your Majesty.'

"They have to make life difficult for us. They have a very heavy book of rules to follow, and if they want to find a problem, they always can. Like if there's a crack in the ceiling, or spices in the processing room. You can't have spices in the processing room in case you make a mistake and put in sugar instead of salt. We have to have them in a little office outside of the processing room and go back and forth for them.

"The inspectors know about what kind of soap you can use to wash your hands but they know nothing about foie gras." The inspector once asked her why she was using Palmolive, which isn't USDA approved, and she said, "Because it's soft on our hands." That answer didn't hold water and she had to switch to a soap from a company called Ecolab, which had been cleared by the USDA.

Any substance used in food businesses under mandatory federal inspection must be approved by the USDA either for use in the product or for contact with the product, according to Daniel Engeljohn, branch chief of quality control and systems development in the processed products inspection division of the Food Safety and Inspection Service. This includes any products used to wash hands, tables, or equipment.

"In order for the facility to use a certain soap, it would have to supply a letter, a guarantee from the manufacturer, saying it's a substance approved by the USDA," says Engeljohn. "We have a very thick book that lists all the approved substances that they can use. They might wash their hands with a substance that might be a poison or something that might adulterate the product. The USDA makes sure whatever they use on their hands that then touches the food is indeed safe for the food." This is not to say that Palmolive is unsafe; its target market is the general consumer, so the soap's manufacturer simply has not requested the USDA to analyze and approve its product for use in food-processing establishments.

The many regulations D'Artagnan has to abide by seem particularly galling because of what she's witnessed a fish company get away with. "Once a truck had just made a delivery and the inspector told me there was debris in front of my kitchen," says Daguin. "We didn't even have a chance to clean it up. As he's telling me this, a guy is dragging a big tuna by the head along the sidewalk and he doesn't say anything to him.

"The inspectors know we can't keep our labels near our spices but they can't tell a pheasant from a chicken. They always say, 'Why does this chicken not have a USDA stamp on it?' and I say, 'Because it's a pheasant, not a chicken.' " (D'Artagnan's pheasants, which are imported from Scotland, are inspected by the Food and Drug Administration, not the USDA. This is because pheasants do not fall under the USDA's definition of poultry.)

According to Engeljohn, the USDA Food Safety and Inspection Service must inspect all domestic and imported meat and poultry products, but the agency's definitions limit meat to the edible portions of "any cattle, sheep, swine or goat" and poultry to chicken, Rock Cornish game hens, capons, roosters, cocks, turkeys, ducks, geese, guineas. Foie gras, an ancient French delicacy whose name literally means "fat liver," comes from ducks and therefore falls under the USDA's jurisdiction.

Ensuring the safety of all other foods, including game such as pheasants, squabs, rabbits, and venison, falls under the province of the Food and Drug Administration as well as to state and local governments. The FDA, for instance, mandates that game captured by domestic hunters cannot be sold because of the iffy sanitary procedures and lack of refrigeration in a hunter's pickup truck.

But while D'Artagnan cannot buy any of its game birds and meats from American hunters, it can buy from hunters in Great Britain, and this is indeed where much of its game comes from. All products imported by D'Artagnan must be simultaneously inspected at the airport by someone from Customs, who is checking for tariff compliance; by Fish and Wildlife, which makes sure that none of the game or fowl are endangered species; and by the Food and Drug Administration, which checks for health and safety. Representatives from all three agencies must be on hand when the shipping seal is broken so that all three agencies will rest assured that nothing was removed from the shipment.

The FDA does not allow fresh foie gras to be imported into this country, and it was a search for excellent domestic foie gras that first brought André to D'Artagnan.

Daguin, daughter of the Michelin two-star chef André Daguin, and her business partner, George Faison, were working at a company that specialized in pâtés when, in 1984, they were approached by a representative from Commonwealth Enterprises in upstate New York. This farm had crossed Pekin and Muscovy ducks to produce Moulards. The livers of these ducks are perfect foie gras—large, creamy blond lobes.

Daguin tasted the liver and said, "No way this was raised here. You smuggled it in from France in the belly of a fish." Canned foie gras is such a poor imitation of the real thing that before the rise of the American industry, some importers would indeed smuggle the genuine article into this country by putting the livers into the bellies of large monkfish.

But, no, the foie gras they had tasted was domestic, and Daguin and Faison went into business as one of the product's distributors. They soon realized "we would die right away" if all they sold was foie gras, and they expanded into poultry and game birds and meats.

Besides foie gras, the order André placed with D'Artagnan last night included four pheasants, six squabs, sixteen saddles of rabbit, six free-range chickens, and eight Pekin ducks.

The Scottish pheasants are wild birds born at the end of each spring and shot in Scotland by hunt clubs in the fall. "The ones who have big domains in Scotland, for a lot of money they let people go there to hunt," says Daguin. "They spend the week or weekend hunting and are allowed to take home only one of each animal they kill. Then the Scottish guys come to me and sell me everything else.

"They are all set up and organized so that on the day of the kill all the animals go to a cleaning place, where they are plucked, packaged, and refrigerated right away. They're put in a refrigerated container, put on a plane, and eight hours later I have them here in Newark Airport."

This shipment is made over the weekend so that D'Artagnan has the wild game in house by Monday morning. "People tend to order it in the beginning of the week before [they want to receive it]," says Daguin. "By Wednesday I know how much I'm going to need for the week after. That's what I order from Scotland, and they send it to me."

The squabs come from a farm in California. "Squabs are one of the hardest things to raise in the world," says Daguin. "They are monogamous. If you are raising ducks, you can put one male with twelve females and he will take care of all the females. But squabs form a couple—one father and one mother—that lasts forever. The mother gives birth to one squab about ten times a year." The baby squabs are killed after twenty-eight days and shipped by air to Newark Airport twice a week.

The rabbits, slaughtered at thirteen to fifteen weeks, come mainly from a large cooperative in Arkansas. Small farmers sell their rabbits to this cooperative, which kills them for use as food and in pharmaceuticals.

The free-range four-pound chickens come from a cooperative

run by the Amish in Pennsylvania. This cooperative hands out day-old chicks and organic feed to small farmers, who are paid to let the chickens have free run of their farms. The cooperative then takes back the chickens after twelve to fifteen weeks, slaughters them, and transports them in ice shavings. The fact that the Amish do not use electricity ensures complete freshness—without refrigeration, the cooperative is forced to ship the chickens immediately.

By way of comparison, a commercially raised four-pound chicken, which is injected with hormones to help it put on weight and kept cooped up inside with lights on twenty-four hours a day to encourage it to eat, is ready in just seven weeks.

The Pekin ducks come from a farm in Indiana, one of the few farms that refrigerates, rather than freezes, the ducks after slaughter. With his dogma of quality and freshness, André will not serve any foods that have ever been frozen.

In a notorious incident in 1979, John McPhee, in a *New Yorker* profile of an anonymous chef called "Otto," reported that "Otto" had eaten frozen turbot and sole at Lutèce. André immediately sent a telegram to *The New Yorker,* demanding a retraction and an apology. He got both. It turned out that since McPhee, at his subject's request, would not disclose the chef's identity, the article had not been turned over to the fact-checking department. The chef's identity did not remain a secret for long. Mimi Sheraton tracked down the allegedly fabulous chef, who turned out to be Alan Lieb, of the Bullhead in Shohola, Pennsylvania, and skewered his restaurant with a critical review. That was the first and last time anyone even suggested the possibility that frozen food, with the obvious exception of ice cream, sorbets, and the long-running frozen raspberry soufflé, would be used at Lutèce.

The Pekin ducks are commercially raised and fed pellets made of grain and vitamin supplements. They are killed after five and a half weeks, when they are becoming adults and changing feathers. Because of this natural molting, they are much easier to pluck. They are then transported in a refrigerated truck and arrive at D'Artagnan forty-eight hours later.

The ducks raised for foie gras live a more luxurious life than those raised for roasting. Ducks for foie gras "must live the life of a deluxe condo," says Daguin. "They have no hormones or antibiotics and eat nothing but corn and some protein. They must have room to walk around at will and they must have air-conditioning. It's true—they need to be cool, and the temperature is controlled constantly."

The word "controlled" again brings Daguin around to the lack of control of the fish industry, something she calls a "dumb thing."

"It's like meat was in the early nineteen hundreds," says the USDA's Engeljohn. "There was no inspection of meat until there was public outcry, like in Upton Sinclair's book *The Jungle*." Published in 1906, *The Jungle*, a realistic portrayal of the inhuman conditions and lax inspections in the Chicago stockyards, helped bring about the passage of the pure food laws.

"There was no mandatory poultry inspection until the sixties, when trading practices were such that there was a demand for that and Congress passed a law to ensure mandatory inspection and that your tax dollars will be used to make sure the product is safe," Engeljohn continues. "There hadn't been any overriding safety concerns [about fish] until recently, when we became more sophisticated about identifying problems, and shellfish became an obvious problem."

There have been many discussions in Congress regarding mandatory fish inspection, says Engeljohn, "but it has not been resolved who should have responsibility for the inspection."

The lack of regulations covering fish doesn't concern André—"I am not a lawmaker"—and it remains his favorite food to cook because "you can do more creative things with it than with meat."

Phil Rozzo, André's main fish supplier, also seems unconcerned. Referring to the government, he said, "I guess they wait until someone gets sick before they do something about it. For mussels, clams, and oysters you need a permit. Each clam is tagged with where it's from, and, in case someone gets sick, they have to keep the tag for thirty days in a restaurant. They're very strict on shell stock. At the Fulton Fish Market they have a health inspector for shellfish, but no one inspects the other fish."

While various consumer groups lobby for fish regulation, Rozzo continues to service many high-level accounts. Today André's fish order includes: four pounds of fillet of sole (from Holland or France), one salmon (farm-raised in Norway or Ireland), four pounds of fillet of sea bass (from New England), five pounds of fillet of red snapper (from Florida), five pounds of bay scallops (from Cape Cod), and two pounds of sea scallops (from Europe).

This is a pretty standard order, but at Rozzo's recommendation, André will often take other fish and turn them into specials. These might be Prince Edward Island blue-shell mussels. "Those are the only ones he'll use because they're clean; there's no dirt in them and they're full of meat," says Rozzo. He makes it sound as if André had specified their geographic origin, but André says, "I don't care where they come from as long as they are the best. He [Rozzo] makes those decisions."

During the season André will also take soft-shell crabs from Virginia and Maryland, crayfish from New Orleans, pompano and frogs' legs from Florida. André tends to use another fish supplier for crabmeat and sometimes for salmon and Dover sole. He uses two fish companies for the same reason he uses two meat companies: so that he can compare their offerings and prices.

Most of the wild domestic fish Rozzo buys have been caught by small boats, which go out in the water for just one day or night. Larger boats go out for three or four days at a time, so that by the time they return to the dock, their catch is already three or four days old.

The boats go out looking for a specific kind of fish, since different nets and lines are used for different varieties. The fish will be sold to distributors on the dock. After they've made their catch, the fishermen radio their distributors and describe the quality and size of the fish. Before the boats even return to the dock, the distributors have called their own customers, and they keep calling until they've sold everything on the boats. They pack the fish in ice and ship them, either by truck or by air. Before the shipment comes in, Rozzo starts calling restaurants to tell them what's on the way.

Fish from New England, Virginia, and New Jersey is shipped by truck to the Fulton Fish Market. The trucks arrive at around midnight and unload at a central distribution center, where all the distributors, like Rozzo, go to pick up their fish.

Rozzo sends its truck down to the market at around three-thirty in the morning. There, the company picks up its expected deliveries and buys some other fish from stands in the market. "We buy stuff we don't need much of," says Rozzo, "like gray sole or scallops still in the shell."

Fish that Rozzo imports directly is picked up at the airport by a company called Norman's Freight. "We tell him, 'We have four boxes at La Guardia or five boxes at Newark'—whatever—and he'll go pick them up," says Rozzo. "He'll be here by four, five in the morning."

The fish gets unpacked and quickly repacked and trucked off to various restaurants. During baseball season the delivery man, a Mets fan, can't walk into Lutèce without being baited for some good-natured sparring with Bill, a Yankee fan.

As he does with all deliveries, Bill weighs the fish and checks it for freshness. He then asks the delivery man "what's doing outside" with the weather. It is turning into a glorious, crisp fall day, but there are no windows in Lutèce's kitchen. Down there, under the bright fluorescent lights, it could be day or night, summer or winter.

Day could easily turn into night, unnoticed, were it not for the importance of hours, minutes, and even seconds to the work these men are doing. Since timing is so important to cooking, the workday here is broken into segments signaled by the buzzers and alarms set by Bill and Joe to time the various dishes they are cooking, baking, or processing.

Both Bill and Joe are very much attuned to what the other is doing. If one man's timer goes off while he is upstairs, or is at a critical point in preparation and can't stop stirring, or has to remove something from the fire at that very moment, then the other will check on the ringing alarm. The same holds true for deliveries. If Bill is very busy, then Joe will check in the merchandise.

Let's leave this kitchen now, where the soft rock music will keep playing and the good-natured bantering between Bill and Joe and the delivery men and the low conversation among the Spanish speaking Ramon, Bernardo, and Guido will continue. Upstairs, through the kitchen window, the back of Jacques's head can be seen as he stirs one of his sauces. Also visible is Juan Taveras, a shy, quiet man who has worked here for twenty-five years and is the *garde manger* for lunch. He will hand the waiters all the cold appetizers and desserts and is currently setting up his station.

We turn right and head for the bar, where Pierre Autret, the lunch bartender, has arrived and is preparing to oversee another important, and highly profitable, part of the restaurant—wines and liquors.

$\mathcal{S}$OLE À LA CATALANE

FOR 4 PEOPLE

4 medium-size ripe
   tomatoes
Salt and freshly ground
   pepper
14 Tb (1¾ sticks)
   unsalted butter, cut
   into pieces, plus more
   as needed
4 small white onions,
   thinly sliced

2 fillets of sole (about
   6 ounces each), split
   lengthwise
2 Tb finely chopped
   shallot
½ cup dry white wine
1 Tb chopped parsley
1 Tb chopped fresh
   chives

Preheat oven to 300 degrees. Carefully cut out core of each tomato, removing a small, narrow plug and leaving tomato intact. Blanch tomatoes in boiling water for a few seconds, drain under cold water, and slip off skins. Cut a lid from smooth bottom of each tomato (opposite the core) and set aside. With melon scoop or spoon, carefully hollow out pulp and seeds from tomatoes, leaving neat shell. Place tomatoes and their lids in small buttered dish, sprinkle with salt and pepper, and set aside.

In small skillet, heat 2 tablespoons butter; sauté sliced onions over medium heat until softened but not browned, 5 to 7 minutes. Spoon onions into tomatoes, dividing evenly.

On a work surface, gently flatten sole fillets, tapping them with side of a wide knife blade. Carefully roll up each fillet, beginning with small (tail) end and with smooth, shiny-skinned surface inside. Lightly butter heatproof shallow baking dish in which fillets will fit compactly. Scatter shallot into dish, then arrange rolled fish fillets over shallot. Salt and pepper fish lightly and pour wine over. Cover with buttered parchment or waxed paper, buttered side down.

Place pan over medium heat and bring almost to boil. Place the pan of fish and the pan of tomatoes in oven. Bake until fillets are just cooked through, 6 to 8 minutes; *do not overcook.*

Remove pans from oven. With slotted spatula, lift each fillet, draining all liquid back into pan, and place each fillet upright in a tomato. Place pan of fish-cooking liquid over high heat and boil until reduced to few tablespoons of syrupy liquid. Reduce heat to very low. Whisk in remaining 12 tablespoons butter, 1 or 2 pieces at a time, adding more only when previous addition has become creamy and smooth. Strain this sauce into small bowl; stir in parsley and chives and season to taste with salt and pepper.

Place each stuffed tomato on warm serving plate. Spoon some sauce over each fillet and around each tomato. Gently replace lids and serve immediately.

NOTE: This is the one of the dishes André cooked to win his cherished Meilleur Ouvrier award in 1968.

8:00 A.M.

All good bartenders have phenomenal recall of people's names. The sociable, chatty fifty-seven-year-old Pierre is no exception. Of all the people at Lutèce—including André and Simone—he is the only one who, from the very beginning, remembered my name. Initially, when I scheduled appointments with André, I would hear him tell his secretary, "Just put down, 'Food writer, three o'clock.' " Thanks to all the positive publicity they've given Lutèce over the years, food writers are top banana with André, who understands the huge power of good press. He always attends to telephone queries and interview requests as quickly as possible.

In the year I spent at Lutèce the relatively unsociable Simone *never* called me by name. Surprisingly, she refused to be interviewed for this book, saying, "This is my husband's business, not mine." After a six-week absence, which I spent writing, she didn't recognize me when I came back to the restaurant, although I had logged in months on its premises. "Yes, madame?" she said, as I smiled at her. Her "Yes, madame?" meant "Do you have a reservation for lunch?"

Catching on with lightning speed, Pierre called out from behind the bar, in one long stream of words: "Hello-Irene-welcome-back-how-is-the-book-going?"

Simone is significantly better at recognizing regular customers—a must in her position as hostess—but even so, Pierre almost always adds his own chorus of hellos to the regulars. A cynic would say that these warm salutations are a necessity, since without them Pierre's role in the food and wine chain at Lutèce could easily be overlooked. Because the bar area is so tiny, it is not the place to come for a drink and a warm chat with the bartender (which is a shame, for Pierre is delightful). The bar functions mainly as a service bar, with Pierre filling drink orders taken by the captains and waiters in the dining rooms. As a result, apart from serving the few customers who order drinks while waiting for tables, Pierre would have little contact with guests, intent on checking their coats and being led into the dining room. That means that were it not for his warm greetings, he would be all too easy to forget at tipping time.

"Hello, Mr. and Mrs. X," he calls. "Hello, Mr. Y." I don't recognize any of the names, but their owners all beam with obvious pleasure at being greeted so warmly. Never mind that the couple behind Mr. and Mrs. X isn't greeted at all and that their excitement at being at Lutèce dims ever so slightly. What can you do? They too can return once a month and tip well. Twenty percent is considered mandatory: 15 percent for the waiters, 5 percent for the captains. The bar and coat-check gratuities are discretionary but quite necessary if you, too, wish to be greeted like a long-lost friend.

Some of the customers have indeed extended offers of friendship to Pierre, especially those who have houses in the Hamptons, a resort community on the south shore of eastern Long Island. Pierre, as he will tell anyone who will listen, has a house in Montauk, a town slightly east of the Hamptons, which he obviously adores. He says that Kathleen Turner has chatted with him at Lutèce about her own summer house, on nearby Amagansett's Bluff Road. Another customer, a wealthy man who has a house on Further Lane in East Hampton, has invited Pierre to go fishing with him. "But I don't go," says Pierre. "We're not in the same class."

I tell him "class" is irrelevant in this country, that my middle-class in-laws are friends of a man who has seventeen live-in servants.

"Maybe living our way is better," says Pierre.

"What do you mean?"

"It would be terrible to have seventeen live-in servants," he says, quite seriously. "You could never walk around your house naked. And, anyway, I'd rather do my own thing in Montauk."

In fact, doing his own thing in Montauk takes precedence over almost anything. He'd even pick Long Island over a tour of the French wine country. "I was in Bordeaux once but I wasn't very interested," he says.

The incongruities between Pierre's job and his own private life abound: Although he dispenses some of the best, and most expensive, wines and liquors in existence, Pierre himself drinks very little. He's known to make a great Bloody Mary but says he's never tasted it because he hates Tabasco sauce. As for that fabulous French food, it may, quite literally, be killing him. To help circumvent the harmful effects of the rich, buttery food that is served to the staff, Pierre takes a prescription anticholesterol pill every day before lunch.

But, still, Pierre takes obvious pleasure in his job. He likes his diverse responsibilities, he likes seeing all the people, and he *loves* the fact that he doesn't have to work Saturdays (rare in this industry) since Lutèce doesn't serve lunch on that day. A different bartender works dinners.

Pierre's route to bartending was a circuitous one, encompassing many other positions in the restaurant industry. He was born in

Paterson, New Jersey, was raised in France, and returned to New York in 1951. Needing to earn a living, he took his first job—as a dishwasher in "an American middle-class" restaurant in Paramus, New Jersey—at the age of seventeen. After a series of kitchen, bartending, waitering, and managerial jobs, and a stint in the army, he became a captain at Perigord Park, which was owned by his brother-in-law. After just seven months on the job, he had a terrible ski accident in which he double-fractured his ankle, and so he couldn't work in the dining room anymore since he'd have to be on his feet too much.

While at Perigord Park, Pierre had worked with its pastry chef, Maurice Bonté, who today owns New York City's Bonté Patisserie. Bonté, a good friend of André's, knew Lutèce had an opening for a bartender (the ideal job for Pierre since he wouldn't have to walk much) and recommended Pierre for it. That was in 1974. Besides tending bar he was put in charge of the restaurant's wine and liquor inventory.

That inventory is quite large—there are forty thousand bottles of wine in stock at any one time. Just as the best department store is expected to have clothing by first-class designers, a restaurant of Lutèce's caliber must have the best vintages from the great châteaus and vineyards. Like window shoppers, however, most of the customers leaf through this large list simply to delight vicariously in what is available. The most expensive and rarest wine is a five-thousand-dollar bottle of 1890 Château Lafite-Rothschild. Customers can read all about the classification and annual production of each vineyard and savor the possibilities. There are choices from twenty-two châteaus offering red and white Bordeaux, three offering just white Bordeaux, thirty-four vineyards offering red Burgundies, sixteen offering white Burgundies, and assorted offerings from other regions, including André's native Alsace. Many prices hover near the hundred-dollar level, but, André says, most customers pick wines closer to thirty dollars. "I don't blame them," he says. "Many times I don't want to [spend a lot on wine] when I go to a restaurant. Once in a while it's your anniversary or you take somebody out where you want to treat them very well, then you take the expensive wine. But not always."

Also, in the same manner as department stores, which display designer clothes and cheaper clothes on separate floors, Lutèce lists American wines and lesser French labels not in its large, thick, and often intimidating wine list but on a separate one-page list. "If we put the cheaper wines in the big book they would be lost," André says. "You'd have one for sixty dollars and then one at thirty or twenty or eighteen dollars. They don't go together, so we came out with this list."

Although Pierre reorders wines when the supply gets low, André is the one who makes the initial selection, and he is also the one who approves the prices, which may fluctuate monthly. Monthly price postings with the New York State Liquor Authority are required to ensure what Richard Chernela, public information officer at the New York State Liquor Authority, calls an "orderly market."

The distribution of wine is policed by state governments as carefully as the processing of meat is controlled by the federal government. "The cliché is that the 'wets' won the war and the 'dries' wrote the rules," says Chernela, referring to the repeal of Prohibition in 1933. "Everybody who touches the stuff needs to get some sort of license or permit from the New York State Liquor Authority, except for the bartender. The strict control stems from the basic belief that alcohol is a drug and it does not enjoy the same freedoms in the marketplace that a pair of shoes would enjoy."

When the United States ended its experiment with Prohibition, the Twenty-first Amendment to the Constitution assigned to the states all powers to regulate the sale of alcoholic beverages within state borders. Under the New York State Alcoholic Beverage Control Law, three levels of alcoholic beverage distribution must be licensed: (1) the distiller or winery that makes the product, (2) the corporation or individual wholesaling the product, and (3) the retailer who sells it to the public. As a retailer, Lutèce, like all restaurants, must have a liquor license, which it renews every three years at a cost of $5,100.

Manhattan's liquor-licensing fee is the most expensive in the country, but at the same time a liquor license is one of the easiest to obtain. Unlike other states, liberal New York does not have a per capita limit to the number of licenses that can be issued. Of course, there are certain restrictions. One is that a convicted felon cannot obtain a liquor license. Another is that a licensee cannot have an interest, "direct or indirect," in an alcoholic beverage wholesaling or manufacturing company. This is intended to prevent monopolies from forming, as they have in England, where, often, a brewery will own the distribution company as well as the pub in which the beer is sold. (Consistent with the intent to prevent monopolies, by the way, is the ruling that you cannot own more than one liquor store in the state of New York.)

Each time Lutèce renews its license it must send a letter to the local community board saying it is doing so. If the community board has any problem with this, it is free to protest the reissuance of the license. Since Lutèce obviously has few, if any, rowdy patrons, the community board has not had any problems with the restaurant's maintaining its license.

Besides its liquor license fee, Lutèce also pays New York State $200 annually for the four French "Lutèce Reserve" wine and champagne labels that the restaurant offers. New York State mandates that the labels of all alcoholic beverages produced outside of New York State must be registered with the state for a fee of $50 per label.

And, of course, there are taxes: The restaurant's inventory of wine and liquor is taxed annually at a cost of about $2,400; the tax on the *license* comes to $425 every year, and there is an annual tax of $250 paid to the Bureau of Alcohol, Tobacco, and Firearms for simply selling liquor.

Lutèce purchases the bulk of its wine from three companies: the Château and Estate division of Joseph E. Seagram, House of Burgundy, and Wine of All Nations. Each of these companies is the exclusive importer for different châteaus and vineyards. Among the top-drawer châteaus and vineyards whose wines are exclusively imported and distributed by Château and Estate are Lafite-Rothschild, Mouton-Rothschild, Petrus, and Margaux.

"[André] will follow the pattern of his wine list," says Maurice Lartigo, senior vice president of Château and Estate. Lartigo personally sells Lutèce all of the wines it purchases from Château and Estate, and he arrives for his meetings with André armed with a huge computer-generated printout of the company's inventory, as well as with the price list it has posted that month with the New York State Liquor Authority.

André comes to these meetings with the restaurant's thick wine list, and Pierre comes with a copy of *Beverage Media*. André simply tells Lartigo which wines he is running out of, and Lartigo reports on the status of his inventory and tells André how many cases of each wine he can have. (When there is a shortage, Lartigo must reserve wines for all of his best accounts.) He also recommends or pans certain vintages, and André faithfully follows his recommendations.

"What André tries to give his customers is continually within certain estates . . . from vintage to vintage," says Lartigo. "He has determined that these estates have fairly consistent quality. The only variations are the vintage variations."

André says wine buying is "a nightmare. It's not like food, where you buy it and you have it. Wine goes out of stock and then you have to replace it with another vintage. It never stops, never ends.

"You don't go out and buy wines just like that," he continues. "A wine cellar has to be built up. We have wines that were bought twenty years ago. It's a very complicated thing. You have to read about it, listen to the specialists and the wine growers on the good years, on the less good years, on the futures. A lot of wine we buy today before it's even in the bottle."

This method of purchasing, referred to as buying futures, is used at Lutèce only for Bordeaux wines. By buying futures, André reserves a certain amount of the wine, not only to ensure he will have it but also to hedge against future price increases.

André usually buys Bordeaux futures about a year and a half

after the annual October harvest of grapes. Most of these wines are consumed six to twelve years after the harvest.

Burgundies and white wines are purchased all year round. Buying, or deciding what to buy, "is nonstop, really," says André. "You read the wine magazines and listen to what this one says and what the other says. You're in contact with the wine growers themselves. When I go on vacation in France [every summer], it's not only vacation. I go to see the wine growers and we discuss it [the quality of a vintage]. I discuss the same thing with the importers. I see if their opinion is the same."

He also makes many of his decisions about Burgundies and white wines after tasting them. "My taste and the taste of another are not always the same tastes. I taste it with my wife, and if we like it, we buy it. Some years you skip them completely. Some years are bad, so I don't buy."

Besides selling, Lartigo is also responsible for buying the Burgundy, Loire, and Rhône wines. Bordeaux purchasing is done by the president of the company. In his buying capacity Lartigo travels to the vineyards three times a year. "I'm gone for about two weeks and I drive five thousand kilometers, visiting maybe fifty producers," says Lartigo. "I taste thirty or forty wines a day.

"I go normally in November, after the harvest, when the fermentation has started, in order to see exactly what type of vintage we are having. You tell that by tasting. In November it is very fruity but you can see by the texture of the wine whether it's going to be a good vintage or not. At that point I have a preliminary idea of what to buy.

"In April I go back to make my purchases. The wine has already stabilized. If we don't like the wine, we're not going to buy an inferior product. In the non-Bordeaux areas they usually have the prices set, and we either argue or pay the prices." The third trip is in the summer and is mainly to buy additional quantities or settle any problems that may have come up.

Once it leaves the vineyard, the wine is shipped to its importer. The importer must be licensed by the federal government to import wine and also needs a broker's permit from the New York

State Liquor Authority. As a wholesaler, Château and Estate takes full possession of the shipment and registers the wines under its brand label. The company then posts its prices with the various state liquor authorities and also advertises them in the monthly magazine *Beverage Media,* to which all the restaurants subscribe. It is via this publication that the restaurants are made aware of monthly price fluctuations and also of any special sales the wholesalers may be offering. The restaurants then contact their salespeople and place their orders.

All wholesale distributors in New York State pay $19,130 for a three-year license to sell distilled spirits, and $981.25 for a wine wholesaler's license, which has to be renewed annually. On top of that, each warehouse must have a separate license and each salesperson needs a permit, as does each truck (a requirement intended to prevent the transport of alcoholic beverages to another state and to unlicensed premises).

When the truck arrives at Lutèce, Pierre logs in the deliveries, making sure that each case contains the right number of bottles. Just as he keeps close tabs on incoming liquor, Pierre keeps close tabs on outgoing wines and spirits as well.

Inventory is the first thing Pierre attends to each day. Every night before they leave for home, the three captains leave Pierre a list of the wines they sold at dinner. From these lists Pierre makes two master lists of his own, one for the whites, another for the reds.

He then takes the actual order slips the captains wrote for each table and checks those individual orders off on his master lists. If no wine was ordered by a table, the captains are required to write "No wine" on the order slip. By the time Pierre has finished his cross-check, the order slips and his master lists for the red and white wines should match exactly.

Next, Pierre checks the master lists against the stock of red wine in the ceiling-high wine rack in the hallway just outside the kitchen and the white wine in the refrigerator at the foot of the steps leading to the prep kitchen. "We strictly control if wine is missing, or if someone forgot to charge for it," says Pierre. "It happens very seldom but it happens."

After verifying that all the bottles from the restaurant's stock are accounted for, Pierre checks the private party list in the kitchen to see which wines he should bring over from the wine cellar for tonight's private party of nineteen.

He asks Jacques if the kitchen has enough liquor to cook with. Jacques does a quick check of the white wine, as well as the brandy, kirsch, and rum used for desserts, and says yes. Pierre takes a one-liter plastic bottle from one of the refrigerators. At the bar he squeezes the juice from twenty lemons into the bottle and returns it to the kitchen, where the juice will be used in various fish and vegetable dishes.

He restocks the drawer behind the bar with cherries, onions, and olives, peels some lemons and oranges, and slivers the peels. He then heads over to the wine cellar—located in the basement of an apartment house a few doors west—where he will check the stock, record any changes in inventory, and reorder some wine.

André has rented four rooms in this dingy basement, whose brick walls have been painted a terrible lime green. To enter, you walk down a narrow staircase outside the building and through a thick metal door. The first room on the right is a locker room for the waiters and some of the kitchen staff. It is also a storage room for linen and mineral water.

The next room, where the white wines, liquor, and beer are kept, is Pierre's office. Against the walls stand dusty metal shelves holding bottles of liquor; the center of the room is completely filled with cartons of white wine and beer. In this claustrophobic space a radio is almost always tuned to the all-news station WINS. The announcer's voice keeps Pierre company as he sits on top of a short ladder at his makeshift desk. The only light comes from an overhead fixture holding three bare light bulbs. Here Pierre oversees the inventory cards, organized by category and label, which show him how much of each kind of wine and liquor is in stock.

The third room, with a more carefully controlled temperature, holds all the red wines. The room is filled with rows of floor-to-ceiling wine racks. The wines are stored according to classification, and signs identifying which are from Bordeaux and which are from Bourgogne (Burgundy) stick out from the top of each shelf.

Across the hall is the fourth room, which serves as a general storage room for miscellaneous items, as well as for cartons of fast-selling wines and liquor bought in bulk when it was offered on special sale. Forty to fifty cases of wines that sell for under fifty dollars a bottle are delivered every week.

There is a popular misconception in the industry that the bar is where restaurants make all of their money, and it's easy to see where this misconception comes from. The markup on distilled liquor ranges from 1,500 to 3,000 percent. The rule of thumb is that the first drink served generally covers the restaurant's cost for the entire bottle. Fifteen to thirty drinks can be poured from one bottle, depending on how the liquor is being served. At Lutèce drinks such as martinis, manhattans, or scotches are $6.00; cognac and after-dinner drinks go from $8.50 to $30.00. The house wine—Burgundy from the vineyard Prosper Maufoux—is $5.25 a glass. As for bottles of wine, their average retail cost is often increased two and a half times when they are resold to customers.

While the bar may be the major profit center for low-end establishments with huge bar areas, it is not at Lutèce. As Cornell's Thomas Kelly says, "The percentage profit is super but the contribution margin is not." In other words, people here eat much more than they drink.

But still, Lutèce patrons drink enough to keep Pierre busy. Following his list, Pierre takes out replacement bottles of those wines that sold last night and puts them in two cartons. Two of the kitchen aides—Guido (who carried Jacques's trays up to the kitchen) and Juan (whom we last saw polishing the silver)—will be over later to carry the wines to the restaurant for Pierre. Every Thursday, before picking up his assigned carton, Guido will have Pierre look up the winning lottery numbers in his copy of *New*

York Newsday. Every Thursday Guido is not a winner and so must carry his carton back to the restaurant. Pierre, meanwhile, remains in the basement, where he meticulously records the changes in inventory, subtracting the number of bottles sold last night from the total on each wine's individual inventory card.

$\mathcal{S}$ELLE DE VEAU PRINCE ORLOFF

1½ lbs. Spanish onions
2 Tb butter
3 cups milk
6 oz. rice
Pinch of sugar
Salt, pepper

3 egg yolks
1 saddle of veal
½ lb. foie gras (cooked)
½ cup heavy cream
½ cup grated Parmesan

Prepare soubise: Peel and slice onions. In a casserole, sauté onions slowly in butter for 5 minutes. Onions should not be brown. Stir in milk, rice, sugar, salt, and pepper. Bring to a boil. Cover casserole and cook in 300-degree oven for 25 minutes. Puree in food processor or pass through a food mill. Mix in egg yolks. Correct the seasoning.

Ask your butcher to prepare the saddle of veal (kidneys removed and rib tips cracked, flanks folded under the saddle to protect the tenderloins).

Pot roast the saddle in 350-degree oven for 50 minutes. Remove the saddle from the pot to a cutting board. With a sharp knife detach the two loins from the bone, cutting out each side of the "T." Cut loins in ¼-inch slices.

Cut the foie gras in very thin slices. Coat each slice of veal with puree of soubise (reserving some) and put veal slices back in place on the backbone, alternating with slices of foie gras. Mix cream with remaining soubise, and cover the whole saddle with this soubise. Sprinkle with grated Parmesan.

Put saddle in a roasting pan. Bake in 375-degree oven until nicely brown, about 30 minutes. Serve with the juice from the roasting pan.

NOTE: An example of a classic dish that is almost impossible to find these days, except at Lutèce.

9:00 A.M.

The three women who handle the bookkeeping, and the phenomenal amount of other paperwork involved in running the restaurant, have arrived in the third-floor office they all share. The room is filled to capacity with cluttered desks, a Xerox machine, and a computer. The sun is streaming in the large window overlooking a few trees and the backs of neighboring townhouses. André's smaller office, still dark at this hour, is separated from this room by a narrow hallway.

At the first desk, pushed against the left wall, sits Jean Delahunty, who handles the billing for the restaurant's four hundred house accounts. These customers simply sign for their checks and are billed monthly. At this hour, Jean is also the one who answers the phone and takes reservations.

At the desk next to her is Odette Ollu, who starts each day by reviewing the computer-generated breakdown of sales and payment received for the previous night's dinner. This breakdown shows the number of people served at each table and the amounts spent on food, wine, and liquor. It also shows if the bill was paid by cash or credit card, and what credit card was used. Odette adds up the sales tax, as well as the tips for the waiters and the tips for the captains. On the breakdown sheets for a recent lunch and dinner, total sales for lunch came to about $4,600 and for dinner to about $13,770. These are pretty standard amounts for Lutèce and bring the restaurant's annual sales in at André's confirmed $4 million plus.

After she's finished reviewing the breakdown, Odette counts the cash and goes to the bank to deposit it, into two accounts, one for restaurant use and the other for sales taxes. Every day, the exact amount owed for taxes is deposited, and payments are sent in monthly. Before leaving for the bank, she will also check that she has enough cash to cover the cashier's needs for today's transactions, as well as for the waiters' and captains' tips. Whatever tips were left for them yesterday on charge slips will be given to them today in cash.

In addition to her financial responsibilities, Odette handles André's correspondence. "I type everything that needs to be typed," she says. "We answer every letter that comes here. There is a lot of correspondence, especially at the holiday season. People will write for reservations from Japan or Australia or other parts of the country."

At the desk perpendicular to Odette's, Reine Dulko sits with her back to the window. She worked here full-time for eighteen years but switched to part-time so that she would be able to take care of her grandchildren. She doesn't talk much, saying, "I'm not good with words but I'm good with numbers." Her proficiency with numbers is important since she pays all the restaurant's bills, keeps the books, and is responsible for renewing the restaurant's numerous licenses and permits, for paying its many taxes, and for handling the payroll. André won't reveal his annual earnings, but a prominent industry analyst told me that other restaurateurs of André's stature earn a solid $500,000 per year.

Showing me the paperwork involved in running a restaurant, Reine pulls a stack of files out of her desk drawer and from them removes form after form, permit application after permit application. Every three years a warehouse permit from the New York State Liquor Authority must be renewed (at a cost of $610). Each year a permit for refrigeration and/or air-conditioning is required by the City of New York Bureau of Fire Prevention ($210), and a permit to conduct a restaurant must be obtained from the New York City Board of Health ($315). Reine shows me proof of service from exterminators, who come regularly. There are copies of inspection certificates from the Board of Health and from a private company, Milton Heller, which the restaurant retains to inspect it for the same sanitary requirements the Board of Health looks for. In its July 1991 report the company found sanitation to be "generally excellent" and the "food temperatures, control and protection" to be excellent. The only problems stated were "ceiling over cooking area becoming discolored and unclean in part" and "ice scoop left on top surface of ice cube machine." Lutèce was instructed to provide a "seamless, readily cleanable container or pan to hold scoop."

There are more inspection certificates for everything from the boiler to the fire extinguishers. All these certificates must be posted, and Lutèce hangs most of them in the tiny, easily overlooked cashier's cubicle across from the main-floor kitchen.

Then there are the taxes: commercial rent tax, filed every quarter; sales taxes, filed monthly; payroll taxes, sent in weekly to cover federal, state, city, and Social Security taxes.

And there is the union. The bartenders, captains, waiters, and busboys are all unionized, and every month Lutèce pays $47 per week per union employee into the union medical plan and $16 per week per employee to cover pensions.

The nonunion employees (kitchen and office staffs) all have Blue Cross, Blue Shield, Major Medical, dental, and life insurance. "That was okay twenty years ago but now it's a problem because it's very expensive," says André. "I think we pay around one hundred and eighty thousand dollars in insurance for the nonunion staff, which is really a lot of money."

At 9:15 A.M. André walks down the flight of steps from his home on the top floor and starts yet another fifteen-hour workday. "Living here," he says, "is a great advantage. I gain a lot of time by not having to commute. I need sleep. I am not one of these guys who can do it with four or five hours."

As he says good morning to the three women, he's thinking: I hope today will be okay. I hope there are no major problems. I hope nobody's sick or had an accident. And, hopefully, I won't have too many calls from suppliers saying something didn't come in.

There are no catastrophes awaiting him in the office, and after answering a few administrative questions, he quickly walks downstairs to the kitchen. He seems to be in a hurry to get out of the office, and later he admits, "I have secretaries, a bookkeeper, and a CPA, but it's not the part of the business that interests me the most.

"Once a year Cornell University comes here with twenty students," he continues, referring to a graduate seminar taught by Kelly. "I give them a little lecture and they can ask me any questions they want. Many times they are business questions, because they are in a business school. They are in a hotel school, and they are taught how food costs go." Usually in a restaurant, whether independent or in a hotel, costs are carefully watched. In most restaurants you wouldn't offer a new dish to customers until you'd figured out exactly how much it would cost you, in terms of ingredients and labor, and what your profit would be. But André doesn't do any of that. If a dish sounds good to him, he makes it and that's it.

"From my answer," André says, "the professor goes nuts. He goes crazy because I work upside down many times for business. But I say, 'Hey, I am thirty years in business and I do good. We make money. We are not billionaires but we make money. So maybe my way of doing business is as good as yours, as good as what they teach you.' "

And just what do they teach students at Cornell's four-year program? Although André thinks the school works solely with charts and graphs and calculators—teaching students how to run restaurants with ideal profit margins of 15 percent and how to keep food costs at an ideal 32 percent of food sales and beverage costs at 22 percent of beverage sales—the truth is actually less cut-and-dried.

I attended Thomas Kelly's first lecture for his Independent Restaurant Management Operations graduate seminar in the spring 1992 semester and was surprised that one of the very first things he said had to do with the hospitality provided in a restaurant, not with numbers. "I teach from a happy, healthy, terrific mode," he told the assembled class of fresh-faced students, all of whom hope to own their own restaurants someday.

In this course, he said, "we are going to basically analyze [restaurants to see if] they are going to provide a generally pleasant experience in order to generate a profit. [You should] not get into the business to make a profit and then consider what the experience should be. [You should work] the other way around. Restaurants don't sell food and beverage for a profit, they market an experience, so we're going to evaluate [restaurants] based on experience." Kelly takes his class to Lutèce because he wants "them to learn the fact that André creates a very enjoyable experience."

Then the class turned to numbers. Kelly projected a page from the 1991 *Restaurant Industry Operations Report,* published annually by the National Restaurant Association. I was surprised to see that the median profit for restaurants was just 3 percent before taxes.

But Kelly said this figure was misleading, since most restaurants that are not publicly traded juggle their figures to show low profits. "If we take the jump to the public sector and examine restaurant chains that are publicly traded, that number will jump up to a median of fourteen, fifteen, sixteen percent," he told his class. "Those are restaurants operated for maximum profit."

After the class was over, I asked Kelly to compare the median

NRA figures with ideal figures and those he assumed Lutèce had. I stress that this is only a guesstimate, because André would not reveal any of this information.

Kelly teaches his students that the total cost of goods sold should be no more than 30 percent of total sales. This would leave their restaurants with a gross profit, before expenses, of 70 percent. The median in the United States is 65.8 percent. Kelly estimated Lutèce's total cost of goods to be 32 percent, which would give the restaurant a gross profit of 68 percent. "André misses by a point or two because of his food costs," Kelly says.

The median food cost among NRA respondents is 36.1 percent. "That's clearly much too high," Kelly said. "Even in a specialty house I don't recommend food costs exceed thirty-two percent." He put Lutèce's food costs at 34 or 35 percent of total food sales.

"Lutèce is higher [than *ideal,* though it is lower than the median] because André doesn't like to raise his prices," Kelly said. "He could charge more, especially on the specials. He goes for expensive ingredients like foie gras or the best fresh fish. He'll pay top dollar and he won't adjust his menu price on a day-to-day basis. The only time he'll adjust is if his accountant yells at him at the end of a quarter, but he won't adjust on a night-by-night basis. There are times when he's just giving away super veal, caviar.

"He doesn't care [about food costs] to the level I think he should. It's hard to criticize a guy who's as successful as André Soltner, but the way we teach it at Cornell, yeah, he's at odds."

Once all the expenses of operating a restaurant are deducted (labor is the highest cost, accounting for a median of 29.4 percent of gross sales), a healthy restaurant's profit is an adjusted 15 to 17 percent, says Kelly, although for accounting purposes this may not be reflected on its statement of income and expenses. As for Lutèce, Kelly stresses that he has never seen any of the restaurant's figures but says, "I'm confident that André has the professional expertise to run the restaurant to generate, if not a taxable fifteen percent, a true fifteen percent profit overall."

Although André claims the business side of the restaurant is not his cup of tea, he is too frugal a person—jumping up to turn out the lights in empty offices, spending virtually no money to spruce up the rest rooms or nonpublic areas, keeping a close eye out for any unexplained price increases from his suppliers—not to have a better grasp of financial matters than he lets on.

However, Kelly says, "André would not be the best person to manage fifteen restaurants. In that sense he does it differently than we would teach it in terms of standardization and recipes printed in the computer and competitive bidding every day and that sort of thing.

"I would be the last one to say André Soltner should sit down every year and write line by line what his food costs and labor costs should be," Kelly continues. "On the other hand, he has a very good accountant. He's a very intelligent man. He knows within a few points what he can afford to be spending within each category. So he manages it more the Cornell way than perhaps he might think that he does."

André insists that he does not. "I am not the type of guy for calculating food costs. I am not a businessman. I am a craftsman and we don't do things like that. Businessmen like Howard Johnsons, they know what everything costs because they are organized that way. But the only thing I know is at the end of the month my accountant says, 'Hey, André. Your food costs went up.' Or he says, 'You had a good month, your food costs is good.'

"I am not a guy who comes from business school. Many times I serve things and I know, I don't know exactly, but I know I lose money. But I have the joy of serving it. I have the joy to cook for them and I make up [the loss of profit] another time. That's my way of doing business.

"We used to refuse so many customers [owing to a lack of space], and every class from Cornell always said, 'Why don't you go bigger?' "—that is, open a larger restaurant or franchise branches of Lutèce across the country.

"I explained, 'Because I don't want more room. I don't want more staff.' Then their reaction and the professor's reaction as well is 'Why don't you raise your prices?'

"I am a craftsman. I don't want to raise my prices. I want to cook, to have customers, to make enough money to pay my staff good and have enough money left for me. But that's it. I don't have the need for so much money."

One illustration of this is that rather than running to the bank with the thousand dollars Malcolm Forbes left him in his will, André gave that money to the three young children of a Lutèce waiter who died of a heart attack some years ago.

He has also turned down numerous highly profitable offers to franchise his restaurant across the country, to license his restaurant's name, and to endorse various food products. In 1987 he told the trade publication *Restaurant Business,* "A few years ago they offered me quite substantial money to go on television and advertise a cake mix. Believe me, I would have to sell a lot of soups to make as much money as they offered me but it's not honest. I don't criticize chefs who do that but I don't agree with it."

André did succumb to commercial temptation in 1988, when he signed a licensing agreement to launch a line of Lutèce dinnerware and appeared in an ad for L'eggs pantyhose. The dinnerware was never launched because André didn't like any of the designs the dinnerware company came up with. As for the pantyhose ad, he did it because "I thought it was funny," and also because it was not an endorsement of a food product.

The ad showed André dressed in his white chef's outfit, holding a whisk and a bowl and looking admiringly at a female model who was dressed up to go out to dinner. The copy read, "She's got dinner L'eggs."

The moment the licensing agreement for dinnerware was announced, members of the food world, always quick to try to knock a king down from his throne, began whispering that Lutèce must be going downhill if André was considering such a commercial venture. Although he denies that they affected him, these rumblings must have hit home and André, more concerned about his restaurant than about making a quick buck, must have reconsidered.

Hurrying down two flights of stairs, André arrives in the kitchen and says hello to Jacques, who, like all the other employees here, calls André Chef. Jacques has been waiting to ask him how much cream of pumpkin soup to make. In the meantime, he's started making today's staff lunch. Armed with André's answer, Jacques now turns to the soup and André walks downstairs to the prep kitchen. After a quick, general good morning to everyone, André takes down the list he left last night and reviews with Bill what has already been done.

"What about the lamb?" says Bill, asking how many saddles to prepare. He doesn't need to explain what he means by "what about." André knows. "Five," he replies.

"How many orders of scallops do you want cut?" Bill asks.

André tells him and then, looking at the list, asks if the *arlequin* is in the oven. Bill nods and André walks into the other room to check on the terrine. "Isn't it on 220 usually?" he calls to Bill, referring to the oven temperature.

"I have it at 300 because it's running funny."

"Put more water in, otherwise it will brown," André says, walking back into the kitchen as Bill goes out and does as André instructed.

Ramon asks André how many more asparagus stalks to peel and André tells him. André scans his "to do" list again and decides that today's lunch special, escalope of veal (veal coated in bread crumbs and Swiss cheese and sautéed) is next in the order of priorities. He starts working on it, shredding a large block of Swiss cheese into a bowl.

"I have to make some pastry," Bill tells me. What he means is that he needs to roll out some already prepared brioche dough that will serve as the crust for the *tarte bressane*. Hearing him, Ramon starts rolling out some pastry of his own instead of doing the asparagus. While Bill makes the finer puff pastry that is used for desserts, Ramon makes the coarser version that is used to wrap the meats and fish that are served *en croûte*.

"See, it's like cat and mouse all day," Bill says to me when he sees Ramon hogging the work space he needs.

Dough here is rolled out using a pastry sheeter, which stands on the far left of Ramon's counter. With just the flick of a switch, it compresses the dough in the same way a rolling pin would. Ramon finishes quickly and Bill takes some brioche dough out of the refrigerator and runs thick squares of it through the pastry sheeter. He lays the sheets in two round tart pans, pressing the dough against the sides of the pans to trim the edges. He wraps the scraps in plastic and puts them back in the refrigerator to use on another day.

As he does this, he asks Joe to make the custard for the *tarte bressane.* Joe nods. He is quite tall and has the slight awkwardness of a young man still growing into his body. Walking through the doorway to the outer room, he hunches his shoulders as if he's not sure whether he'll fit under the door frame. Bill is much smaller in stature, and the disparity between the size of his hands and Joe's hands is regularly noted during the course of a workday. Now, for example, as Bill lists the ingredients to be used for the custard, he says, "It's five eggs, three-hundred-fifty grams of sugar, a quart of cream, and four of my handfuls of almonds or two of yours."

At 9:45 a buzzer goes off, signaling Bill that the *arlequin* terrine should be ready. Bill checks on it, but seeing that it is still slightly soft, he resets the timer for another ten minutes.

The phone buzzes and André is summoned upstairs to take a telephone call from a customer. In the meantime, Bill begins making the individual beef Wellingtons. He trims the fat off the filets mignons and weighs each portion on a little scale, allotting 160 to 180 grams per serving. He weighs the meat, instead of just relying on his eye, because, he says, "it makes for consistency and to cover myself if the chef comes down and says, 'That looks big,' or 'That looks small.' I can show him how much it weighs."

Bill wraps white twine around the outer edges of the filets mignons so that they will hold a circular shape and brings them upstairs for Jacques to sear.

André has returned to the kitchen, and seeing that Guido is momentarily unoccupied, he says, "You can start [cleaning] the gambas and oysters when you have nothing to do."

From the doorway to the smaller room Joe calls, "Chef?"

André looks up and sees a knee-high girl and a slightly taller boy standing in front of Joe in the doorway. André hurries over and picks the girl up, gleefully hugging her tight and then raising the laughing child high above his head. "Where were you?" André says. "I haven't seen you in a long time." The little girl lives in the neighborhood and comes in from time to time to get cookies. This is the first time the little boy has come with her.

André puts the girl back down on the floor and says to both kids, "You want a cookie?"

They nod. André pulls down two large plastic containers filled with cookies. He hands each child a cookie and then fills two plastic bags with cookies.

A third child, an older girl, walks in. Seeing her, André gets a third plastic bag and fills that with cookies too.

"Why haven't you come in?" André says to the knee-high little girl.

"I haven't had a chance," she replies solemnly, munching on her cookie.

"You made this?" she asks André after she swallows.

"Yes," André responds, his eyes twinkling.

"It's very good."

André smiles and asks, "Why aren't you in school?"

"It's staff-development day," says the little boy.

"What's that?" asks André.

The kids shrug. Bill, who has been watching this scene unfold, turns back to his work saying, "Sounds like a golf day to me." The kids leave and André says, "She comes and we don't even know from where." He was obviously delighted to see the child but he turns serious again as a lobster delivery from New York Fish House arrives. Bill takes the lobsters out of their bag, puts them in a white plastic box and weighs them as a group. "Lobsters lose water on their way here," he says, looking at the weight written on the delivery slip. "These ten lobsters lost three quarters of a pound." He tells the delivery man this but the man just nods and doesn't adjust the weight on his copy of the delivery slip. Bill records the weight loss on his copy of the slip and says, "We'll adjust the weight when we pay the bill."

MÉDAILLONS DE VEAU
AU FROMAGE À LA CRÈME

FOR 2 PEOPLE

1 cup grated Swiss
  cheese
1 whole egg
1 Tb flour
Salt, pepper
Dash of nutmeg

$^1/_8$ cup milk
4 veal médaillons
1 Tb butter
$1^1/_2$ oz. Madeira
$^3/_4$ cup heavy cream

Cheese batter: In a bowl, mix cheese, egg, flour, salt, pepper, nutmeg together. Add milk and stir.

Coat the médaillons with the cheese batter. In a frying pan, brown the médaillons in butter about 3 minutes on each side.

Remove the médaillons to a warm platter and deglaze the pan with the Madeira.

Whisk in the cream and simmer until it starts to thicken and becomes velvety in texture.

Correct the seasoning and pour sauce around the médaillons.

Serve with fresh noodles.

10:00 A.M.

ndré scans his "to do" list again, deciding which dish to work on next, and answers the ringing phone. The call is from a woman who has just started a spice company and wants to know if she can come and show André her offerings.

"We don't use so many spices," André says into the telephone. "Are you speaking of spices for pâté? . . . Sure, it's no problem. I'm always here. . . . Next week. Any day but Monday. Just come by."

He tells me suppliers are always trying to sell to him so that they can go to other restaurants and say, "We sold these to Lutèce." There is not an ounce of self-aggrandizement in his tone. He states it simply as fact and it is indeed a fact. When a food-importing company called Flying Foods was launched, André was the first chef the company's principals contacted. As *The New York Times* reported in 1983, Flying Foods "went to Lutèce first, on the theory that if André Soltner bought fish from them, everyone would."

The phone rings again. It's Phil Rozzo calling to tell him about some fish that have just come in. "Whole turbot? From where are they? Yeah. Then it's great. I take it. . . . Salmon from Maine? Put in one salmon for me." André hangs up and writes down this order in the order book.

During the year I spent at Lutèce, the thing that surprised me most was how often decisions about what to offer as dinner specials got made at the last minute and what an important role the suppliers played in these decisions.

To me, the logistics of feeding so many people, and trying to predict what they would order, seemed overwhelming. I would have thought everything would have been planned way in advance, the way a hostess plans a dinner party. Indeed, the menu is set and the lunch special is planned a week in advance, but the creation of the dinner specials is centered around phone calls such as the one André just received from Rozzo.

"Cooking for me is preparing something new every day," André says. "If I had to prepare the same menu for ten years I wouldn't see the point. There's no excitement in that."

Even the daily lunch specials are sometimes subject to unexpected changes. "Sometimes, at the last minute, something won't be available," says André. "Let's say I wanted sturgeon but the boat broke down and so the fisherman couldn't go out and get sturgeon. I have to get something else."

The phone rings again, and this time it's a customer calling to discuss the menu for an upcoming dinner party. "How are you?" André says. . . . "Your cholesterol stinks? Well, come see us."

He laughs, listens for a moment, and then says, "What do you think about a fish soup? A small portion. Not too much. . . . Then salmon. . . . Lamb is nice and veal is nice. . . . I will make you a nice rack of lamb and caramelize it. And I'll make half portions of asparagus. Then we need something on which we can write 'Happy Birthday.' "

The phone rings again and André puts the customer on hold. It is one of the restaurant's captains calling from upstairs. The two waiters who came in at ten to set up the dining rooms don't know where to put a group of twelve that is coming for lunch. André answers him in French and then goes back to his customer on the other line.

"You know what we do?" he says. "I'll make you a Grand Marnier soufflé and we'll write the names on it. . . . Three names? Okay. Give me the three names." He writes the names down on his little pad of white paper. Then he says, "Maybe a chocolate tart for after? The kids would like that. How about the wines?" He notes down the choices. He is using a tiny, worn-down pencil stub hanging from a long piece of white twine next to the phone. This tiny pencil reflects the Lutèce philosophy that nothing be wasted.

A woman with short red hair arrives carrying a carton of tomatoes. She is Lucky Lee, a co-owner of Sunrise Sun-Ripened Tomatoes, Inc. She and André exchange pleasantries, and after she leaves he tells me the story of that company. Ten years ago, Lucky gave up a show business career to spend time with her terminally ill grandmother in Florida. There, she and three of her six siblings went into the tomato business by chance. Fed up with the poor quality of the tomatoes they found, even in Florida supermarkets, the kids went to a local "U-pick" field, where they could choose their own.

At first they picked just for themselves. Then they decided to pay for a visit to their mother, who lived and worked in New York, by bringing a van load of tomatoes with them and selling them in the city. Word of the tomatoes' beauty and taste spread through the restaurant world, and over the next several years the siblings rented bigger and bigger trucks. Today they own their own tractor trailers.

Later, Lee tells me she first knocked on Lutèce's door three years ago. "I'd heard André was a living legend. His attention to detail and consistent dedication to what he does is what brought me there. I knew that someone who cared that much about what he did and someone who was there all of the time to take care of his customers [would want the best possible tomatoes]. Many times you find owners and chefs who are not there taking care of business. They spend half their time there and half the time flying all over doing promotions.

"I remember the first time I brought him a box of tomatoes, he looked at it and said, 'I haven't seen tomatoes like this in twenty years.' I wanted to fall over. Here's someone I had tremendous respect for and to get a compliment like that just bowled me over. He had won a big award in France for a dish he did with tomato and fish and he said these tomatoes would enable him to be able to do that dish again."

Lee has come to know André well, but still, she says, "I can't get him out of that restaurant. I do tomato tastings at the James Beard House and tomato talks. On a number of occasions I have asked him if he could please be my guest chef and do the food. His dedication to the restaurant is so strong that he will not take the night off."

The phone's intercom buzzes. André is told a customer is waiting upstairs to see him. He walks upstairs and into the bar, where the man introduces himself and says he's hosting an upcoming dinner party here and wants to plan the menu and the wine. (He had called earlier in the week and made an appointment to meet with André.) André shakes his hand and the two sit down at one of the small tables at the bar, behind the captain, who is taking reservations.

Today the captain is Roger Benjamin, and he's set himself up at the large front table, with a phone, the reservations book, a deli cup of coffee, a pack of cigarettes, and an ashtray. He will pencil in the reservations on a large pad. He has added a clean page to the reservations book, an add-a-page binder, for the corresponding day a month from now. A fresh page is added daily, which prevents the captains from mistakenly making reservations any further than one month ahead.

This system once saved André from a lawsuit. One summer, on a Monday, he received a phone call from a man complaining that he'd had a Saturday dinner reservation and when he got to the restaurant he found the restaurant was closed. The man said he'd had to go to another restaurant and had a bad meal, and that Lutèce was to blame and had to pay for his dinner.

André explained that it was impossible for him to have had a reservation for that day because "we don't have a book that we can make a mistake. We add one page every day and when we are closed on Saturday we don't add a page."

The man sent a registered letter saying he was taking André to court, but in the end, André's lawyer brought the man in, showed him the add-a-page binder, and, as André says, "straightened him out."

Roger answers the frequently ringing phone, repeatedly saying, "*Bon jour,* Lutèce. . . . For when? . . . For how many? . . . Your name? . . . That will be fine. . . . Please call the day before to confirm. . . . Thank you." He writes down the name of the person making the reservation and the number of people in his or her party. Every day, Simone will review the next day's reservations list and decide who will sit where.

Meanwhile, the customer is telling André, "The dinner is for my friend's sixtieth birthday party. For my fortieth birthday, some years ago, my friend said that as a gift I could pick any restaurant in the world to have a meal in and we would go. I picked one in Paris. Now my friend is celebrating his sixtieth birthday and I made the same offer and he picked Lutèce."

I expect André to say he's honored, but instead he says, "What did you have in Paris?"

The man recounts every dish and then says, "My friend is extremely knowledgeable about food and wine, so I want to do something extraordinary, guided by you. Maybe after we plan the menu three or four of us could come over and have it in advance. Is that okay with you?"

"I'm not too excited about that," says André. "When you have something the first time you're more excited and it tastes better to you than it does the second time. I don't recommend it. I will make you dinner but I don't recommend the same courses."

"No. I've eaten here. I know the food. I accept your recommendation."

Keeping a very businesslike demeanor, André says, "I like to start with a pre-appetizer. Fish soup or half a quail boned and stuffed with mousseline of foie gras."

"That sounds wonderful. We're off to a good start."

"Then a fish dish. I could make for you a small bass with the head cut off. It's filleted. I put the two fillets together and attach only the tail. Baby sea bass with a mild sauce."

The man nods. "The baby sea bass sounds wonderful and it will keep the portion size down."

"Then, before the main course, I like to break it up with maybe a sorbet."

"I'm not a big fan of sorbet. Let's skip that."

"Okay. You were speaking of veal. [The entrée at this man's fortieth birthday party had been veal.] I can make—" The captain interrupts André to say he has a call from a food writer.

André talks to the writer briefly and returns saying, "I can make saddle of veal Prince Orloff. You take the saddle of veal, braise it, and cut it back [slice and reassemble] with truffles and foie gras. It was first made for Prince Orloff, you know, the Russian prince. He liked it. It depends what kind of food your friend likes, modern or classic."

"Classic."

Ah, *classic*. That word conjures up an entire world of food, going back to the eighteenth century. Defined literally, classic French cooking "embraces the supreme French dishes, those elegant, inspired creations of the great chefs that have stood the test of time," Craig Claiborne and Pierre Franey write in their book *Classic French Cooking*. The cuisine first blossomed in the palaces and châteaus of pre-revolutionary France and came to full flower in the days of the great French chefs Marie-Antoine Carême (1784–1833) and Georges Auguste Escoffier (1846–1935).

"This cuisine is more demanding and more precise than any

other," according to Claiborne and Franey. "It has its own traditions, techniques and requirements. Stocks, sauces and garnitures
are required in most classic recipes. Since the traditions are so
strict, French chefs employ a kind of culinary shorthand—'serve
with a Madeira sauce,' or 'stuff with a chicken mousse,' or 'garnish
with puff pastry crescents' —and each understands the other—
perfectly."

The roots of French cooking lie in Italy. When fourteen-year-old
Catherine de'Medici married the future King Henry II of France in
October 1533, she brought her cooks to France, and the Florentine
cooks, in turn, brought along such delicacies as sweetbreads, truffles, and artichoke hearts.

As French cuisine evolved, truffles and mushrooms were frequently used as subtle accents for meat, roasts were served in their
natural juices, fish were prepared in a stock made from their trim-
mings, and butter was substituted for meat fat in pastries. Food
was no longer disguised but appreciated for its true flavor.

The French take full credit for the creation of an important component of dining—the restaurant. Although today it seems that
restaurants have been around forever, the first restaurant in the
modern sense of the term was opened in Paris in 1765. "Someone
put out a few marble tables in a ground-floor room," says *The
French at Table*, by Rudolph Chelminski, "and began serving
bouillons, chickens, various egg dishes—known as strength-giving
restoratives in those days . . . to a clientele of passing pedestri-
ans." Outside this establishment hung a sign that said, in Latin,
"Come to me, all of you whose stomachs are in distress, and I will
restore you." Initially, the place was referred to as a "restaurat"
(for a place where you eat restoratives) and over time the word
became "restaurant."

Restaurants soon sprang up throughout Paris and large provin-
cial cities as Napoleon's rule brought widespread affluence and
luxury to France. The old aristocratic households with their elabo-
rate kitchen staffs had disappeared, and many of the talented
cooks who had served these households found jobs in restaurants,
or opened places of their own.

As restaurants developed, so too did French cuisine, particularly with the chef Carême, who brought French cooking a step closer to the classic cuisine we know today.

Carême was born the sixteenth child of an impoverished stone-mason in a Paris slum in 1784, shortly before the French Revolution. When he was eleven his father told him to leave home and make his own way in the world. Carême knocked on the door of a simple restaurant, and its owner took him in and put him to work the next day. The boy remained there for a few years and then was apprenticed to the owner of the finest pastry shop in Paris. There, he created replicas of antique structures—temples, fountains, forts, towers, and classical ruins.

When Carême began his career, all the dishes at banquets were set out at the same time on tables, in no particular order, and diners ate as much as they wanted from whatever dishes were within reach. Carême was the first to direct waiters exactly *where* to put dishes on the table so that entrées and side dishes meant to be eaten together would be within arm's reach. Today this type of service, in which large numbers of dishes are displayed simultaneously, making a show of their massed beauty, is called *service à la française.*

After Carême's death in 1833, food in France continued to be ornate and extravagant. Then, at the end of the nineteenth century, as life became more industrialized and democratic, the chef Escoffier came to the forefront. As Claiborne and Franey write in *Classic French Cooking,* Escoffier called for food to fit an age "when life is active, when a thousand worries of industry and business occupy the mind of man, and he can devote only a limited place to eating well."

Escoffier, born October 28, 1846, picked his profession at a time when a restaurant cook held a lowly position in the social hierarchy. Many years later he was named an officer of the French Legion of Honor, the first chef to be so distinguished. By the end of Escoffier's career, and largely thanks to his efforts, a cook was a respected personage.

Escoffier invented scores of outstanding new dishes (including the one André cooked to win his Meilleur Ouvrier de France award), streamlined the art of decorating food, reduced menus to manageable proportions, speeded up service, and organized his kitchen along more efficient lines. Rather than having one chef prepare an entire meal, he initiated an assembly-line process, with specialty squads responsible for one category, such as sauces, fish, meats, side dishes, soups, and pastries. This sensible method of working in the kitchen continues to this day.

During Escoffier's time *service à la russe,* the Russian style of serving courses in succession to the individual diner, supplanted *service à la française.*

In the nearly hundred and fifty years since Escoffier, many other cooks have exerted their own creative influences. They created a modern school of French cooking known for inventiveness, simplicity of presentation, a reluctance to use heavy sauces, and open-mindedness toward exotic ingredients.

Had André's customer said his friend preferred modern cooking, André might have suggested shrimp with saffron sauce or sautéed fillet of bass with stewed tomatoes. But since he requested classic cooking, André makes another suggestion: "Or we could take the veal, boned and rolled, with veal kidneys."

"What do you recommend?"

"Saddle Orloff. Named for a prince, it's a special dish. I think your friend will like it."

"Let's do the veal Orloff."

"Then let's change our first course," says André, "to maybe a fish and crab soup. It would make a better balance with maybe a side dish of salad. This is all for the same price." The man agrees.

"How about dessert? It's your friend's sixtieth birthday. I can make individual soufflés and write his name on them."

"Wonderful. Chocolate."

"He likes chocolate?"

"Yes."

"What about Grand Marnier or vanilla with his name written in dark chocolate sauce? It looks better."

"Okay." He gives his friend's name to André, who writes it down on his pad.

"Now the wine," says the man.

"We have a big selection. It all depends on how much you want to spend."

"I want to spend less than we're going to spend," the man says with a nervous laugh.

Taking him up on his cue, André says, "Twenty-five or thirty?"

"We have to do better than that."

The man's tone is patronizing. I'm annoyed by it because André was simply offering what the man seemed to want, but André doesn't bat an eye. He simply gets up and retrieves the huge leather-bound wine list. The man opens the list. Leaning over, André points to the Tokay d'Alsace and says, "I have here something very good and you don't have to spend a fortune. It comes from my village so I am prejudiced. You will not find it anywhere else. It's President Nixon's wine."

"And Margaux was his red, so it can't be all bad," the man says.

"But Margaux is not in this price range."

The customer leafs through the book. "Do you ever let people bring their own wines from their cellar?" he asks.

"No." While some restaurants let customers bring their own wines—as long as they pay an uncorking fee—André is adamant in his refusal. He's asked some of his best customers to check their wines in the coat room, refusing to serve them until they handed over their bottles.

André walks down the hall toward the dining room and returns with the single sheet listing the cheaper French and American wines and recommends a magnum of a red Bordeaux. (He later says that if people need some guidance in selecting a wine he often goes by their age. "If he's rather young [which this man isn't], I go rather on Burgundies than on Bordeaux because Bordeaux are a little lighter wine. They're easier to digest. In France we say you drink Burgundy up to age fifty, then after that you drink Bordeaux. Now the Bordeaux people don't go with that too much and the Burgundy people don't go with that either, but that's what people say.")

The man agrees to the Bordeaux and André excuses himself to see if he has it in stock. There is no phone in the wine cellar and so André walks up the block to find out himself. He pounds on the locked cellar door and Pierre, who has been sitting at his desk listening to WINS and doing inventory, lets him in.

Together, André and Pierre look at the file cards and see that, yes, the wine is in stock. As André quickly strides back to the restaurant, he tells me he "loses a lot of time" planning parties. It is a spectacular crisp fall day but André takes no notice of the weather, even though this is one of the few forays he will make outside. He is capable of spending day after day indoors, without ever leaving his building.

Back in the bar, the customer, who has been reviewing the wine list, says, "How about the '79 Latour?"

"I have to check," says André. He runs back to the wine cellar, where Pierre tells him he has two magnums.

Why magnums? "Because red wine is almost always better in magnum bottles," André says. "It ages better. The more quantity you have together, the better becomes a wine. And, for a party, it impresses."

Back at the restaurant, Roger says, "Phone, Chef. *The New York Times.*" A reporter is calling to interview André for an upcoming article on sweetbreads.

"Hi," André says. "Yeah . . . yeah . . . Okay. There's no secret but a few steps are important. You blanch them and then put a plate on and weight them for a few hours or overnight so that all the blood goes out. The second thing we do . . ." He describes the steps and then says, "It takes a lot of work." The reporter then asks for recipes and André describes a few of the ways he prepares them. He listens to another question and then says, "I like them very much . . . Well, that's a difficult question. What do I like about them? Their taste and texture . . . We sell an average of six to eight portions a day."

While André is on the phone, the man planning the dinner party tells me he's with a Los Angeles–based law firm that opened an office in New York. "People from California always ask me, 'What's the best restaurant in New York?' and I always say, 'Lutèce.' They say, 'How could it be the same place for so long?' and I say, 'I don't know how. But it is.'"

The prime reason is because André has been the chef for the entire time. He later tells me that unless the owner is also the chef, a restaurant is very vulnerable. "The demand for chefs is so high," he says. "Other restaurants are always trying to hire people away from me. If the chef leaves, which he will, then the restaurant changes and that's bad for the restaurant."

After André finishes with the phone call, the customer makes a final selection of wines, choosing both a white and a red. He then asks if André could serve Lafite cognac at the end of the meal. André doesn't stock this cognac, but he tells the customer he'll get it for him.

With that, the customer leaves and André hurries downstairs, where Bill is on the phone telling a friend of his who works at the Gotham Bar and Grill to wish his fiancée a happy birthday. "I couldn't find your home phone number," he says. He stiffens slightly when he sees André and says, "I can't really talk now."

He hangs up and tells André, "That was Scott."

"How are they?" André asks.

What he's really asking is how business is at the Gotham. Understanding this, Bill says, "They dropped twenty covers [people] for lunch but dinner is the same. They're still doing good."

André nods and looks at the bacon Bill is cubing for the lamb stuffing. "Don't make everything," André says, referring to the bacon. "Two thirds, about."

A meat delivery arrives from Piccinini and André checks the meat against the invoice. It's all there and it's perfectly fresh. André signs the delivery slip and puts this meat next to the DeBragga and Spitler delivery, which is still out on the counter, waiting for the noon arrival of the butcher.

Another delivery man arrives carrying a carton filled with duck and game from D'Artagnan, and André checks that in too. Bernardo then takes the ducks and starts cleaning them. After he's finished, four of the ducks will go in the combi oven for twenty minutes. Most entrées are cooked to order, but this would not be possible with ducks since they take too long to roast. There are always eight ducks in the refrigerator; four are partially cooked every morning, since André is confident that at least that many will be ordered at dinner. If those four ducks sell early in the evening, then a few more will be partially cooked at that time. Not precooking too many helps André avoid waste.

Joe takes some scallops out of the refrigerator, smells them to make sure they're fresh, and starts slicing them. They will be used as the garnish for the *arlequin* terrine.

Suddenly from the wall behind Joe's counter come sounds like balls being rolled down the stairs. It's Juan Espinal, the silver polisher, running downstairs. "I thought it was a busboy," Joe says, seeing Juan. "All the busboys come down the stairs like that." Joe tells me Juan is a "bulwark for miscellaneous jobs. He's strong as an ox. He'll carry two hundred pounds of flour on his head and while he's coming in he'll be dancing."

Joe looks up and sees a Hispanic man tentatively peeking into the kitchen. "Can I help you?" Joe asks. The man wants to talk to André about a job, but despite Joe's exhortations, he won't come into the kitchen. He waits by the combi oven and André goes out to see him. The man's voice is heard saying, "Hi, Chef. Do you remember me?"

André responds with a simple declarative, "No." The kitchen staff gets a big kick out of that and Bernardo stops spinning the lettuce long enough to repeat both lines: "Hi, Chef. Remember me?" Then he lowers his voice as he booms out, "No," and laughs.

The man quietly asks André if he has any jobs available. André just as quietly says that he has nothing right now but that the man can leave his name and number and André will call him if something opens up. André returns to the kitchen with the man in tow. He writes down the phone number the man gives him and says, "You're not working now?" The man shakes his head no.

The phone rings and André answers. "Yeah. That's me," he says.

He listens to the caller and then angrily says, "It's impossible, this charity. Every day I get five or six calls. Everyone calls me. I can fill my restaurant this way every day. I don't think I will be able to help you this year." And he hangs up.

The job hunter leaves and everyone goes on with their tasks, with Bernardo still chuckling, "Hi, Chef? Remember me? No!"

André opens a few packages of duck breasts that will be smoked for an upcoming day's special and casts a quick eye around the kitchen to see how everyone's work is progressing. He takes in Bill working on the stuffing for the lamb, Juan helping Guido clean the large shrimp, Bernardo cleaning the ducks, and Ramon cleaning salmon. Joe has temporarily disappeared into the refrigerator. Although he expects his staff to work autonomously, André is always there, always casting a quick, watchful eye on what they are doing and how they are doing it.

As André finishes opening the packages of duck breast he asks Bill if they have enough wood left to smoke the duck. Whenever their supply runs low, André brings a small basket of it back with him from the woods behind his house upstate.

"Yes, Chef," says Bill.

Joe, meanwhile, has reappeared carrying a large plastic container full of lobsters. He picks them up one by one, and sees which ones are fighters and which make the weakest motions. The weaker the motion, the older the lobster. He picks the weakest ones to cook today.

As he does this, a busboy noisily clatters down the stairs and gets to work slicing chunks of butter from a large, slightly softened block. He presses the chunks into small white bowls and covers each with a small circle of waxed paper printed with the word "Lutèce."

Upstairs, two waiters have set up the dining rooms and the rest of the waiters and captains are arriving for work.

$\mathcal{B}$REAST OF MUSCOVY DUCKLING

FOR 2 PEOPLE

2 Muscovy duckling　　　　　*2 large chopped shallots*
　breasts　　　　　　　　　*1 Tb brandy*
Salt, pepper　　　　　　　*½ cup red wine*
½ Tb oil　　　　　　　　　*½ cup chicken stock*
¼ lb. butter

Bone and trim fat from the 2 duck breasts. Season with salt and pepper. In a skillet, sear the duck breasts in ½ tablespoon of oil and ½ tablespoon of butter. Brown them on both sides for about 8 minutes (6 minutes on skin side and 2 minutes on the other side). Transfer them to a cutting board and let sit for 5 minutes.

In a skillet, sauté the shallots in ½ tablespoon butter. Deglaze with brandy and red wine. Reduce for 2 to 3 minutes. Add the chicken stock. Boil to reduce the sauce by half and thicken with remaining butter. Season to taste and strain.

Cut the breasts diagonally into thin slices. Pour sauce into two serving dishes. Arrange the duckling slices on the sauce in fan shape and garnish with sautéed egg noodles with fresh julienned vegetables.

11:00 A.M.

There are three captains, eight waiters, and three busboys employed at Lutèce. Unlike the kitchen staff, which works a straight eight or nine hours, the dining-room staff works a split shift. This means they work lunch, have a long break, and then the same people work again at dinner.

Most of them arrive at eleven, but one group—one captain, two waiters, and one busboy—arrived at nine forty-five. While the captain took reservations, the early arriving waiters and busboy set the dining-room tables for lunch with linen tablecloths and napkins and Christofle silver. The "Malmaison" Christofle pattern chosen by Lutèce was created in 1909; it was also selected by Princess

Caroline of Monaco, the king of Nepal, the shah of Iran, and President Anwar el-Sadat of Egypt for his private plane.

In addition to the silver, a place setting includes Minners Designs glassware, each piece hand-blown in Virginia; Noritake china bread plates; twelve-inch Woodmere porcelain entrée plates —larger than the standard ten-inch dinner plate to better showcase the food—and a bud vase with a few red roses. The waiters use the instructions Simone has left in the reservations book as a guide to how many places to set at each table.

The waiters also set up a small service table, at the center of each station. These tables hold extra silverware for each station and are used to carve chicken and fillet sole, for example. They are also where the orders for each station are left so that the waiters and captains can easily refer to them.

Roger Benjamin, the captain taking reservations today, has worked here for seventeen years and in the course of that time has served many famous people. "In the beginning," he says, "I would ask them for their autographs, but not anymore."

After seeing so many of the rich and famous, he's come away with some strong impressions. Gregory Peck, he says, was the worst tipper; Frank Sinatra was the best. "Frank Sinatra always paid cash. He'd have a wad of bills in his front pants pocket. He'd tell his guests he had to go and make a phone call and would walk around the restaurant and tip everybody."

As for personalities, he says Joseph and Robert Kennedy were "mean," while John and Ted Kennedy were "okay, normal." So are Richard Nixon and Mick Jagger. "He's a nice guy," Roger says of Jagger. "He looks at the menu and asks, 'What's this?' like a normal person. You explain it to him and he understands and he orders. The others are off, crazy. Dalí would ask you what time it is and you'd say twelve and he'd say, 'Is that before or after?' You wouldn't know what he was talking about. And Dalí would never sign his check because he was afraid someone would sell his signature."

Woody Allen and Mia Farrow (who had their first date at Lutèce) would "come in and stare at each other." "He's weird," Roger says, imitating Allen sitting on the edge of a chair, chewing with small motions of his jaw, and nervously glancing over at Mia Farrow. "Maybe he's just so smart that I can't understand him. I can't understand his movies either."

André is more close-mouthed about any negative impressions he may have of his more famous customers. But even given his own celebrity status, he is somewhat star-struck and keeps a beautiful leather-bound autograph book with signatures of personalities in a diverse range of fields: Moshe Dayan, George McGovern, Eugene McCarthy, Judy Collins ("I am happy here," she wrote. "Your fine cooking, your sense of flavors and ambience; they have given us great pleasure"), Danny Kaye, Burgess Meredith (who signed once in 1973 and once in 1986), Charles Lindbergh, Lillian Hellman, Rusty Staub, Joanne Woodward and Paul Newman, Henry Kissinger, Frank Sinatra, John Lennon and Yoko Ono, Isamu Noguchi, Woody Allen (whose handwriting looks exactly the way I'd imagined it would, round as a schoolboy's), Rod Stewart, Bill Cosby, Mick Jagger ("The most delicious food in New York. Thank you"), Shirley MacLaine, Ed Koch ("I had two desserts"), Prince Rainier of Monaco (who wrote, all scrunched up and in a straight line across the top of the page, in French: "Marvelous cuisine. Brava and thank you"), Diana Ross, Claudette Colbert, Rex Harrison, Jackie Gleason ("To André, The best undoubtably" [sic]), Isabelle Adjani and Warren Beatty, John McEnroe ("Thanks for one of the finest meals I've ever had"), Itzhak Perlman, Omar Sharif, Mickey Mantle, and Robin Williams ("Chardonnay gone tomorrow. *C'est fantastique. Merci à jous pour tous*"). Also, tucked inside the book is a handwritten note from Katharine Hepburn, thanking André for sending over an order of escargot to her nearby town house.

Bill Cosby has sent flowers, and last Christmas former President Nixon sent a wreath, which an obviously thrilled André hung in the restaurant for a few weeks. "That tells you how close we are," he said. "He is a former president. He has other things to do than think of Lutèce. But on Christmas he had a thought for us and sends us a Christmas wreath."

Do these famous people have any preferred dishes? "No," says André. "They're like anybody else. One day you feel like eating fish, the next day you feel like eating beef. I go to see them and I say, 'What do you feel like eating?' And we go from there."

While André won't reveal negative aspects of any regular or famous customers, he's very vocal in his feelings about the interloping newcomers who don't show up for their reservations. "Reservations are a vital problem," he says. "People don't respect them. We have only twenty-nine tables and sometimes have six tables that are no-shows, especially on weekends. Our profit margin is not that great. If we lose three or four tables, our day is lost.

"I'm normally a smooth, nice guy but I have a real arrogance for that [making sure no tables are left standing empty]. We ask people to please reconfirm the day before. If they do, that means they're coming. If they don't reconfirm we cross them out. If they show up we say, 'Sorry, we asked you to reconfirm.' It's the only way for us to fight back. I would like to be nice about it but it doesn't work."

Once André got so angry at a man who never showed for a confirmed reservation for six people that he had to get revenge. "I waited until three o'clock in the morning and called Waldorf Tower, that's the phone number he left when he made his reservation, and asked for the gentleman. They rang at his suite and he came on the telephone and I said, 'Well, I am the owner of Lutèce and you have a reservation and I, with my whole staff, am waiting for you. Should we continue to wait or will you cancel your reservation?' "

André laughs as he recalls the man's horrified, "No, no, no, no, no. Don't wait! Don't wait!" response.

The reason Lutèce will not take reservations more than one month in advance is that so many people don't keep them. "We've had people try to make reservations two years in advance," André says. "A lot can happen in that time. They can get divorced or die. A lot of people change their plans. One month is a fair amount of time."

There are other high-end restaurants that religiously keep a few tables open for good customers or friends who want to come at the last minute. Lutèce does not. Anyone who calls in time can get a table here, and once you're in you can expect to be treated well.

"Most New York restaurants of that caliber treat you like scum if you're not part of the 'in' group," says John Axelrod, a lawyer and businessman from Boston and an investor in New York fashion designer Carmelo Pomodoro's business. He's been eating at Lutèce since 1971 and says, "The only difference between the way they treat me now and the way they treated me when I first came in is that now they know my name."

André certainly knows the name of Marc Sarrazin, Jr., but when this son of his best friend called to say he wanted to propose to his girlfriend at Lutèce that night, he was told, "Sorry, we're booked. No exceptions." Finally, Sarrazin junior asked his father to call on his behalf. He did and in the end convinced André to squeeze in a new table for two.

Ariane Daguin of D'Artagnan, the restaurant's game and poultry supplier, has had a different experience. Sometimes her suppliers and her accountant, knowing she sells game and poultry to Lutèce, ask her to call Lutèce on their behalf. She's tried, but the only response she's ever gotten from André has been "You know better than that."

"Most restaurants keep two or three tables that they can shuffle at the last minute," says Daguin, "but not André. He is too straight for that. It's the Protestant in him."

Sometimes good customers get bent out of shape because Lutèce won't make exceptions for them, but at least it doesn't play games like those I witnessed at La Grenouille. I spent some time there, observing the behind-the-scenes goings-on as preliminary research for this book. One night the maître d' was out and Charles Masson, Jr., who was running the restaurant with his mother, Gisele, was filling in for him. He was standing by the front door when a man wearing a polyester suit and tie walked in alone and asked for a menu. Charles gave him one. After reviewing it, the man said, "Is it difficult to get a reservation here?"

Without giving the man a direct answer, Charles said, "When would you like it for?"

The man once again asked, "Is it difficult to get a reservation?"

"When would you like it for?" Charles repeated.

"How about for tomorrow?"

"What time?"

"Six."

Even though Charles later told me he "knew the room was wide open," he made a great show of looking in the reservation book. "We still have a few tables free at six," he said.

"It would be okay still if I called in the afternoon, no?" said the man.

"It should be."

After the man left, Charles said, "You never tell them it's easy to get a reservation. Then they think [the restaurant] isn't worth going to. Malcolm Forbes taught me that lesson when he asked me to illustrate a poster for a balloon race. After I gave it to him he said, 'What about admission?' and I said, 'I didn't know you were charging admission.' He said, 'When we had it free, it was a rampage. People destroyed the grounds. When we started putting admission on it, that kept the bad people away. If you make people pay for something, they pay attention to it. They have more respect for the grounds.' If people think reservations are hard to come by, they'll respect the restaurant more."

La Grenouille plays games too when assigning you to a table. "We don't give them the table they want because then they won't come back because they think it's too easy," says Charles. "We may seat them in the front, but we won't seat them at the table because they'll say to all their friends, 'Oh, La Grenouille is too easy.' People want what they can't have."

And whom does La Grenouille want and not want in its dining room? "We don't want people who ask, 'How much is dinner?'" says Charles. "We don't want lowlifes in the dining room. There are so many things that can ruin someone's experience of the restaurant. If the couple next to them isn't happy and start having a fight, there's nothing you can do about it, but the next time they call you for a table, you can say you're fully booked. It may seem silly, like you're turning away business, but you're really protecting your business."

Once you get on La Grenouille's "out" list you remain out. When you call for a reservation, the maître d' will simply tell you the place is booked.

When I ask André if he has an "out" list he says no, although he has turned a few people away. One was a freeloading food writer. "Once I got a letter from a writer from Chicago," he says, "and the letter said that he goes all over the world to the best restaurants, and he asks us to serve him the best bottle of wine we have in the cellar and he writes a story about that. So I wrote him back that the best bottle of wine stays in my cellar unless he pays for it. Very truly yours. I never heard from him again."

Another person he refused to serve was a man who made a big stink over being seated upstairs. After hearing his complaints, Simone immediately told André this customer wasn't happy. "I went to him with a big smile," says André, "and said, 'Look, sir, I know you are not happy here, but I promise I will make you a great meal.'

"He was not nice," André continues. "He said, 'Oh, I don't want to be up here. Look around who else is up here. You have only peasants.'

"I said, 'You call my customers peasants? That's it. I don't cook for you. I want you to leave. There is no law that I have to cook for you.' I told the captains and waiters not to approach their table and twenty minutes later they left."

André confronts difficult customers directly, before things get too far out of hand. "We are in a business where we like to please people, but some people are difficult. They come for a fight, not for enjoying. With these touchy people we do as much as we can that they are pleased. We don't want anyone to go out unpleased. But sometimes it just doesn't work.

"We feel pretty soon that they will be a problem by many things," he continues. "Many times it starts at the telephone. We feel they will be difficult by the way they speak and act. Sometimes we write a little sign by their reservation that means 'be careful' and many times we are right. We don't treat them differently but we are alert, on our guards, which is a bad way to start. We had a lady a few years ago who made a reservation and we felt that there could be a problem.

"So when the lady came in, we had a lot of room. It was a couple and they came very early. When the lady came in she said to my wife, 'I was here two years ago. I wasn't pleased. You tell the chef he better be good today.'

"My wife said nothing because we don't want to fight. We are in the service business, where it has to go smoothly. She maybe said, 'We'll try our best,' or something like that and then she told me what they said.

"As soon as they were seated they called the captain and said they didn't like the table. The captain said, 'No problem. Let me ask Madame Soltner.' She said they can be in the garden room, and they moved there. Once the woman sat down she told the captain, 'I was here two years ago and I didn't like it. You tell the chef he better be good today.'

"So first my wife told me and then the captain came and told me the same thing. They were here ten minutes and changed tables and said two times I had better be good. So I thought, Here we don't go further. That's enough. I have to do something now because there will be no end. So I went to the table and introduced myself. I said, 'I am the chef and the owner. Look, lady, you are here ten minutes. You said when you arrived that you didn't like it two years ago and then you didn't like the table and then you sit down here and you say again to the captain that you didn't like it here two years ago. I think it would be much better for both of us if we straighten things out. I am here and you are here. If you will come one third to me I will come two thirds to you. If you think you can do that, then I will do my best to make your evening pleasant, to serve you good. But if you think you cannot do that, then I think you better go.'

"She was very shocked and she said, 'Oh, no, no, no. Don't be upset.'

"I said, 'I am not upset at all, but I don't want you to be upset.' She stayed and everything went fine, but if I hadn't stopped it right there it would have gone on all night."

Then there was the German banker who was having a party for thirty people. That night, he came a little earlier, telling André he wanted to make sure everything was fine. "I said, 'Everything is ready,'" says André. "Then suddenly he said, 'What deal do you give me?'

"We had already set the price. I said, 'No deal.' He didn't get upset, nothing. He said, 'Okay, but then you offer us the champagne when we have dessert.' Champagne for thirty people. That's when I really get mad. I speak German and he had a heavy German accent. I said to him in German, 'Sir, everything is ready, but it doesn't matter. You have no deal and you have no champagne and you take it or you leave it.'

"The guy was like stone for a second; then he looked at me and said, 'Sir, I like your attitude.'

"I said, 'Fine, you have dinner then. We'll serve you.' We served them, they paid, and everything was fine. But, you know, you go to Bloomingdale's and the price is twenty dollars, you pay twenty dollars. They don't tell you, 'We'll give you a pair of socks on top of that' or 'We'll give you a twenty percent discount.' But people think in a restaurant it's different. After so many years here in New York we don't usually have a problem because everybody knows how we do business."

11:30 A.M.

The noises of the kitchen—the chopping, whirring, washing, and clanging—cease and blessed silence descends as the staff eats. Every day the dining-room staff sits together in the upstairs rear dining room while the kitchen staff, including André, will grab a plate in the upstairs kitchen and eat in there. If time allows they sit down, but most of the time they eat standing up. The cooks eat on one side of the kitchen, by the stoves; the kitchen aides on the other side.

Today, down in the prep kitchen, Joe is making incisions in the parboiled lobsters that will soon be roasted to order in the upstairs kitchen. His incisions will allow the waiters to easily remove flesh from the lobster before serving it. "This isn't a place where we give people a bib and a crusher," says Joe.

André repeatedly tells Joe to go have lunch. Joe replies, "Yes, Chef," but he keeps working until he's finished the lobsters. Finally, he and André head upstairs to the kitchen, where Jacques has set out a hot buffet lunch for the staff. They help themselves and sit down with the rest of the chefs on chairs that have been temporarily borrowed from the dining room. The other chefs have finished eating and the other kitchen workers are eating standing up.

Even though Joe pauses between bites long enough to tell André about a recent dinner he had at Peter Luger with the other cooks, both he and André finish their meal in less than ten minutes.

While her husband ate, Simone stood at her hostess station, reviewing the reservations list, refreshing her memory as to who will be arriving and where they are to be seated. The staff lunch is over and Pierre is at the bar; Mirielle is at the coat check; Jacques is at his stove, where he has been joined by two young cooks—Henry Meer, who cooks the fish, and Denis Fitzgerald, who cooks the hot appetizers and prepares the garnishes. Juan remains at the *garde manger* station, and another man named Juan has arrived to wash pots and cooking utensils and to man the dishwasher. The prep-kitchen staff has returned downstairs to continue preparing the food for dinner and some of the food for tomorrow's lunch.

In the dining room, the wait staff, dressed in their uniforms (tuxedos for the captains; short black jackets, vests, and long white aprons for the waiters and busboys), stands at the ready, waiting for the doors to open and the first customers to arrive.

$\mathcal{F}$ILET MIGNON EN CROÛTE LUTÈCE

FILET MIGNON IN PUFF PASTRY

FOR 4 PEOPLE

4 filets mignons, about
* 5 oz. each*
Salt
Freshly ground pepper
1 Tb peanut oil
4 slices of uncooked
* fresh foie gras, about*
* 1 oz. each, or 4 slices*
* of terrine of foie gras*
1 Tb unsalted butter
2 shallots, peeled and
* chopped*

6 oz. mushrooms,
* washed, chopped*
* coarse*
Flour for flouring the
* work surface*
1 lb. puff pastry (Lutèce
* makes its own but*
* you can use frozen)*
1 egg, beaten with a
* little cold water*
Sauce périgourdine
* (recipe follows)*

Salt and pepper the filets mignons. In a skillet, heat the oil over high heat, and sear the filets mignons for 1 to 1½ minutes on each side, depending on the thickness of the meat. Remove the meat from the skillet, set aside, and let cool.

In the same skillet, over high heat, sauté the foie gras (or terrine of foie gras) for ½ minute on each side. Salt and pepper the foie gras while it is in the skillet. Remove the foie gras from the skillet, set aside, and let cool.

In a sauté pan, over medium heat, melt the butter. Add the shallots and sauté for 1 minute. Add mushrooms, salt, and pepper, and continue sautéing until all the liquid has cooked off and the mushrooms are dry. Set the mushrooms aside and let cool.

On a lightly floured work surface, roll out the pastry in a sheet

$^1/_{16}$ of an inch thick. Cut out 8 rounds, each the size of a filet mignon plus a $^1/_2$-inch border all around.

Place 4 of the pastry rounds on an ungreased pastry sheet. Place 1 filet mignon at the center of each round. Place a slice of foie gras on each of the filets mignons. Spread $^1/_4$ of the sautéed mushrooms on each slice of foie gras. Brush the exposed edges of the pastry with a little of the beaten egg.

Place 1 of the remaining pastry rounds on each of the filets mignons. Firmly press the overhanging edges of the top pastries to the exposed edges of the bottom pastries. Brush the top pastries with the beaten egg. Refrigerate for at least 15 minutes on the pastry sheet.

Preheat the oven to 425 degrees.

Trim off the excess pastry, leaving a $^1/_4$-inch border of sealed pastry around each filet mignon. Place the filets mignons on the pastry sheet, on the center rack of the preheated oven, and bake for 12 minutes—until the pastries are golden brown.

Serve with *sauce périgourdine* (recipe follows) and garnish with any vegetable.

$\mathscr{S}$AUCE PÉRIGOURDINE

FOR 4 PEOPLE

3 oz. port wine

¼ cup cognac

⅛ cup truffle juice from
a canned black truffle

1 oz. black truffle,
chopped

1 cup veal stock (recipe
follows)

2 Tb unsweetened butter
(¼ stick)

Salt

Freshly ground pepper

In a saucepan, reduce the port and cognac by one-fourth.

Add the truffle juice, truffle, and veal stock. Bring to a boil, reduce heat, and simmer for 10 minutes.

Stir in the butter. Add salt and pepper to taste. Simmer 10 minutes more.

VEAL STOCK

YIELD: 1½ QUARTS

2 lbs. veal bones, cut in
small pieces

2 carrots, trimmed,
peeled, washed, and
cut in ½-inch pieces

2 stalks celery, peeled,
washed, and cut in
½-inch pieces

1 medium onion,

peeled, and cut in ½-
inch pieces

1 bay leaf

1 sprig thyme

5 sprigs parsley

2 garlic cloves, unpeeled

1 Tb tomato puree

2 cups dry white wine

3 quarts water

Preheat the oven to 450 degrees.

In a roasting pan, roast the bones in the preheated oven until they are nicely browned—about 20 minutes. Add the carrots, celery, and onion to the roasting pan, and roast for 10 minutes more.

Transfer the bones and vegetables to a large pot. Pour off the grease from the roasting pan, and then scrape any browned material that adheres to the roasting pan into the pot.

Add to the pot the bay leaf, thyme, parsley, garlic, tomato puree, and wine. Add 3 quarts of water. Bring to the boil and simmer, uncovered, for 3 to 4 hours. Regularly skim the grease and scum from the surface of the liquid during this time. If the liquid reduces too much, add water. Strain through a fine sieve.

Lunch

Before the doors of Lutèce open, allow me to digress for a minute to illustrate how bad service can ruin a meal, no matter how good the food, and keep you from ever returning to a restaurant again.

In December 1990 my husband took me out to dinner for my birthday at The American Hotel, a pricey restaurant in Sag Harbor, Long Island.

I was in the middle of researching this book and had recently read about proper food service. For instance, one textbook told me that "to the uninitiated, it might seem very simple to arrange food nicely on a plate. Actually, in a refined service, food is arranged according to particular rules that are followed the world over." For example, meat is always placed at the lower part of the plate, at six o'clock. A piece of cake or pie should be served with the point facing toward the guest.

I'd never known this and didn't see its importance. What difference did it make if my meat was at twelve o'clock or my pie pointed toward three o'clock? None, unless you were trying to set your watch accordingly. But now that I know these facts about food arranging, whenever I entertain I make sure to place the meat on the lower half of the plate and make sure the cake slices point toward their consumers.

An article in *Vogue* noted that when you set a table, the tines of all forks should be level with each other and that spoons and knives should be lined up at the base of their handles. It also said that soup is a beverage and must be cleared and served from the right like other beverages, an exception to the serve-from-the-left, clear-from-the-right rule. Coffee cups and tea cups are placed with their handles at four o'clock, and the wineglass goes above the point of the dinner knife. Women are to be served first (including the hostess), then children, and finally men (the host is served last).

These are points that all fine restaurants are aware of. Now I was aware of them too but I wasn't thinking about any of them as we arrived at the restaurant. All I wanted was to have a good meal and to enjoy my husband's company. He was already slightly put out by the restaurant's policy of not accepting reservations more than a day in advance. Lutèce's policy of no more than a month in advance made sense to us but The American Hotel's policy seemed extreme.

But we'd gotten a reservation and my husband, who wanted to make sure my birthday celebration was perfect, was doing his best to forget about the unnecessary uncertainty the restaurant had forced us to endure. Both of us were ready for a nice dinner out. Our expectations were high not only because it was my birthday but because we knew we would be spending a significant amount of money for this meal. But as long as the food was good and, on the whole, it was a positive experience, we were prepared to pay.

We gave the hostess our name and I was impressed when she

nodded knowingly, said, "Yes, for two," and checked our name off on the reservations list without needing to hunt for it. That made me feel less anonymous, as if not being able to make reservations until the day before had resulted in more personalized service. The restaurant scored points but then lost them when the hostess led us to a round table that had been set for four. With such a strict reservations policy, a table set for two should have been awaiting us.

After she'd cleared the extra place settings the hostess handed us menus and left. Before choosing this restaurant, we had come by and looked at the menu so we already knew what we would order.

But ordering was not a speedy proposition. Even though we were ready, there was no sign of our waiter. A busboy brought over a plate of small olives (their saltiness makes you thirsty and their oils stimulate the appetite) but didn't fill our water glasses. I couldn't help thinking of a passage in the *Vogue* article that mentioned that some restaurants tell their waiters not to give customers water because they hope the customers will purchase a mineral water or a drink from the bar.

A solid ten minutes later, our waiter finally came over and asked us if we wanted anything from the bar. My husband asked for the wine list and water. The waiter brought both and disappeared again without listing the specials or mentioning whether anything on the menu was not available.

He left us alone again for quite some time. I don't know how it is for other people, but I am most conscious of how well a restaurant is run in the moments before I order, and this waiter gave us plenty of time to take things in. I noticed that our table was set incorrectly. The empty wineglasses were not over the points of the knives as they should be but over the tines of the forks which, by the way, were not lined up evenly. We joked about what a scandal this was. We didn't care, but we noticed. And then we noticed that the chair at the table across from us was terribly scratched and pitted and saw that another twosome was being shown to a table set for six. The hostess started clearing the extra silverware but the two complained that the table was too large for them. They were then shown to a table for two that had just become available.

Our waiter didn't tell us the specials until he came over to take our order, and when he did, he had an inordinate amount of trouble remembering what they were. When he got to the end of the list, he told us they were out of a soup listed on the menu. This didn't concern us since it wasn't one of the items we were planning to order.

We ordered two radicchio-and-arugula (spelled "rugula" on the menu) salads with Gorgonzola and walnuts ($6.25 each), and I ordered the beef tournedos with foie gras ($28.50), while my husband ordered the grilled Black Angus steak ($25.00). Birthdays are the only occasions on which cholesterol counts are forgotten in my usually health-conscious family.

The waiter wrote down both orders but not until then did he say, "We're out of radicchio so the radicchio-and-arugula salad isn't available."

I said, "That's okay. Just serve it to us with arugula."

"No," he said. "I really don't recommend it. The flavors are not the same without the radicchio."

Although I insisted that I really didn't care about the radicchio he countered that the salad was not available. I said, "Why? Are you out of arugula too?"

He said no but held his ground, and finally we ordered different salads. Mine was warm chèvre on toast with arugula ($6.95).

He disappeared into the kitchen and soon returned, looking quite sheepish, and said, "We're out of the foie gras." He handed me the menu again but none of the other entrées appealed to me. The waiter said, "You can have the same beef and I'll shave some truffles on top for you."

Plain shaved truffles didn't sound particularly appetizing but I remembered that one of the specials had been beef with a truffle-butter sauce. "How about that one?" I asked him.

"That's what I meant," he said.

I ordered that dish. I was slightly disappointed that they didn't have any of my first choices but André had told me that he runs out of things at Lutèce too. André's theory is that it's better to run out and order things fresh every day than to have things left over. Even though I understood that this is unavoidable, I was still disappointed, especially since my disappointment could have been avoided had the waiter been up front with us in the beginning, telling us what the kitchen was out of, and recommending other dishes. We should not have been left with the menu for so long with no information on what foods were not available.

But I shrugged it off and turned to my husband, wanting to forget about the restaurant's problems and get on with our pleasant evening. A few minutes later our waiter, looking even more sheepish, was back at the table, again empty-handed. We looked up. As a joke I almost said, "You're out of wine," but I remained silent, since the restaurant was known to have the largest wine cellar on Long Island.

"We're out of the wine," the waiter said.

Now I was angry. At the end of the night we were going to hand over more than $150 for this meal and we weren't going to be served anything that we had wanted. But we didn't complain. We simply chose another bottle of wine. By now, however, our conversation was not about personal things but about the restaurant and how was it possible for it to be so poorly stocked.

Things got progressively worse. Since the restaurant was calling attention to itself, we couldn't help but notice that the wine was served from the side the food should have been served on, and vice versa. The waiter put my husband's plate down first. My "warm" goat cheese was cold. I ate it without complaining. But when my beef, too, arrived cold, I sent it back. For $28.50 for the entrée alone, I figured I should at least have a warm meal. The beef came back hot but I was unable to eat it since the waiter had taken my fork with the first plate and had not replaced it.

As my warm beef got progressively cooler, we searched the room for our waiter, who was nowhere in sight. We waited and waited but to no avail. Finally we asked another waiter for a fork. He rolled his eyes in sympathy, making us feel that our waiter was known to be a screw-up. The second waiter brought me a fork and dashed off before I had the chance to ask him for some pepper. I ate half my meal before I saw our waiter again and asked him to pepper the meat. He missed and peppered the vegetables instead. I let it go.

The entrée was good and the wine was good and we settled down to be good sports and try to have a pleasant evening. After our plates were cleared I turned and saw a waiter (not ours) coming out of the kitchen with two desserts, one of which had a candle in it. I leaned over and kissed my husband, thinking that these desserts were for us, since in the past four years my husband had always gone to the trouble of calling in advance, ordering a slice of chocolate cake for us to share and asking that the cake be served with a candle. The desserts, however, were for the table in front of ours, where a woman was also celebrating her birthday.

We laughed about this coincidence. Then our waiter came over and said, "I want you to know I'm very sorry about how your meal went, and because we were out of so many things that you wanted, I'd like to offer you dessert on me." My husband and I looked at each other. I knew for sure that he had called in advance for a slice of "surprise" birthday cake, and he knew I knew, but we listened to the dessert selections. I ordered a delicious-looking apple tart someone at the table in front of ours was eating, and my husband ordered a slice of chocolate cake. The waiter left and my husband, who cares a lot about making special days special, said, "I called this morning and told them to bring out a slice of chocolate cake for you. That waiter has no idea that it's your birthday."

I told him to forget about it, but he got up and went to talk to the hostess. A man who seemed to be the owner was standing next to her, and my husband told him he'd called in advance to ask for a slice of cake with a candle in it, but that our waiter seemed to know nothing about it, since he just took our dessert order. My husband asked the owner to please put a candle in my apple tart.

Sitting at the table, I saw the owner march into the kitchen. In time, a four-inch-square cake with a "Happy Birthday" inscription on it was placed in front of me by our waiter, who made no reference to the "free" apple tart and chocolate cake we had just ordered. This was the fourth instance in one evening of my desires being thwarted: no radicchio, no foie gras, no wine, and no apple tart. Staring at the cake, my husband said, "I asked him to put a candle in your apple tart, not to bring out a completely different dessert."

I felt terrible for my husband, and when he wondered if the waiter was bringing the apple tart as well, I said, "I hope not. I'm full." I blew out the candle, we each had just a bite of the cake, which tasted like cheap chocolate and wasn't worth the calories.

Our desired desserts never did arrive. The bill did, however, and on it was a twenty-dollar charge for this junky, unwanted, unordered birthday cake. That was the last straw. My husband, feeling terrible that my birthday celebration had deteriorated to the point that all we talked about was how terrible the service at this supposedly fine restaurant was, took out his charge card. He wanted to cut our losses and get out of there as fast as we could.

I, however, called the waiter over and told him we refused to pay twenty dollars for a cake that we hadn't ordered. "And," I said, "what happened to the free desserts you promised us?"

Giving free dessert or wine, by the way, is a ploy often used by dishonest waiters to increase their tips. They figure that if they give you something for free, you will tip them more generously. I didn't think our waiter was up to that kind of trick, because there was a fixed service charge here of 17 percent, which we paid, chumps that we are, even though the service was terrible. Yet I later heard someone at a table next to us saying they wanted to tip the waiter extra on the side because he had given them something for free. In cases like this, the waiter benefits but the restaurant loses since the cost of that item comes out of the restaurant's pocket.

My question made our waiter swallow hard. He said he had gotten "chewed out" by the owner for not remembering that it was my birthday. He said he'd gotten confused because the table in front of ours had a birthday too. He said that he'd offered us free desserts without getting clearance from the management first, and now that the owner knew we had been given dessert, he would have to charge for it; otherwise he would lose his job.

"All right," I said. "We're not going to make you lose your job but we're still not paying twenty dollars for a whole cake we didn't even order. Charge us for a slice."

In the end, the waiter took the cake off the bill. My husband reviewed the new check and handed his charge card to the waiter, who disappeared into the kitchen with both, only to reappear a minute later, with his by-now-familiar sheepish look, to say, "We don't take charge cards. We take cash, checks, or, if you want, we can send you a bill."

We gave the waiter our address and then asked to see a copy of the menu again, specifically to see if we'd missed a note on the card policy. But, no, no mention was made of that fact. Nor had my husband been informed that the restaurant didn't accept charge cards when he made our reservation.

What should have been a special evening was ruined because the disappointments and slip-ups in service made us focus on the restaurant rather than on each other. This experience made me appreciate the seemingly flawless service at Lutèce even more.

"It looks very easy on the outside but there is a lot of tension behind everything," says André. "The main thing is that the customer doesn't feel the pressure. Sometimes customers go to a restaurant and they can feel the pressure and that makes the customer very uncomfortable."

★　★　★　★

Lunch service at Lutèce begins as an elderly man and woman present themselves to Simone. She greets them the same way she'll greet most of the customers, "*Bon jour, monsieur, bon jour, madame.*" The couple respond in French and nod hello to Pierre, who greets them warmly by name. After Mirielle takes their coats, Simone shows them to the dining room, with a brief pause at the kitchen window for them to say hello to André. He's standing in the kitchen sipping a black iced coffee and reviewing the day's mail. Among the letters lying on the counter are a few from people interested in working for him; one from a group of students at the Culinary Institute of America, thanking him for letting them film a video in the restaurant; a report from Milton Heller Food Sanitation, the company retained by André to inspect the restaurant regularly for any sanitary flaws; and a long letter from a family of shallot growers in Washington State, who ship André a case of shallots every other week. In the letter they tell André about their crop and about their new grandchild. Enclosed is a picture of the baby.

Most of his customers don't realize that like all chef/owners and executive chefs, André will leave most of the cooking to the cooks who work for him. Here today there are four: Jacques will cook the meat, Henry the fish, Denis the garnishes; and Juan will prepare the salads and cold appetizers. But the customers ignore the other cooks and focus on André, seeing a world-famous chef in a world-famous restaurant standing in his kitchen seemingly waiting for *them,* ready to cook for *them.*

And André will perpetuate this impression by going out to the dining room and saying to his regular customers, "Today I can make for you . . ." This is his standard line, one that purposely makes it sound as if he will head for the kitchen and cook whatever he's recommended to these customers. In reality, these specials have been assembled in advance and are available—in fact, are recommended—to everyone else in the restaurant.

"Most of the time I ask my people to do it, to prepare this or that," André says of the orders he takes and of any special requests the customers may have. André's role in the kitchen is more that of a supervisor, and also a pinch hitter. He fills in wherever he's needed, wherever anyone needs help. "I cook whatever needs to be done," he says. "I am comfortable everywhere."

Since he does indeed spend most of his time at each meal in the kitchen, and since the food is the most important aspect of the restaurant for him, André, along with the other cooks, has donned a toque, or chef's hat. In many other French restaurants his seniority would be immediately apparent by the height of his hat. He would have the tallest, followed by the *sous-chef,* who would have the next tallest, and so forth. Here, however, everyone's hat is the same size. "I'm a very liberal guy," says André. "I buy the hats and I buy the same size for everybody, mine and theirs, so when we are on work there is not much hierarchy. We sweat together and I don't feel comfortable with a too-high hat." André does, however, have a fancier jacket than the rest of the kitchen staff. Since he will make frequent forays into the dining room, his jacket is slightly more formal than the others. It has cuffs on the sleeves, the buttons are covered with fabric, and there are four little ventilation holes under each armpit.

Just as seeing André is meaningful to the customers, so too is seeing his customers important to André. As he's said many times, cooking is like a love affair. André works as hard as he does to please people, to make them happy, to get glowing praise from them at the end of the meal.

At the beginning of every meal, in anticipation of giving and receiving love, André can be found glancing through the kitchen window to see whom he and his excellent staff will be pleasing today.

It is easy to differentiate between the customers who know André and those who don't. Most of the latter look into the kitchen but, if they happen to meet André's gaze, tend to shyly look away. If André is momentarily occupied, they stare and stare at him. Other newcomers follow Simone to their tables without even glancing toward the kitchen.

The regular customers, on the other hand, smile and say hello; some shake hands through the kitchen door's little window. André has developed solid relationships with many of these customers, and some are eager to repay the warmth André has bestowed on them over the years. For example, one customer noticed that the restaurant's computer monitor threw off a great deal of glare and said it shouldn't be used without a screen. The next day the customer came back with a screen in hand and installed it.

Smiling at the customers who stop to say hello, André, who's always ready for a good joke, shakes their hands and repeatedly introduces me to them as the new chef. Upon leaving, some of these customers will congratulate me on having created their excellent meals, and André will beam as I say thank you.

André's dentist, Sam Cohen, has a story to tell about André's sense of humor. Some years ago, around 1982, André broke a tooth and went to the dentist's office with the jaw of a lamb. "See if one of these teeth fits me," André instructed him.

At the restaurant André reserves his humor for the regular customers he knows will appreciate a joke, and he spends much more time listening than talking. He greets the regulars with a standard "How are you?" and many give him long answers. For instance, a man from Pittsburgh who frequently travels to New York on business and has been a patron for twenty-five years tells André he hasn't been here for five months because his wife crushed her ankle and knee in a car accident. André offers his sympathy. In the dining room the man tells his captain that he recently turned sixty-five and has retired. He receives what seem to be heartfelt congratulations.

Now Simone walks by the kitchen and stares determinedly at André, willing him to look up at her. But André is reading the letter from his shallot grower and doesn't notice her trying to make eye contact with him. Finally she hisses "Chef!" through the window. He looks up but she doesn't say anything and remains expressionless. Two seconds later fashion designer Bill Blass appears. The two men greet each other heartily and Blass follows Simone to his table in the front room, where smoking is permitted and where he will lunch with John Fairchild, chairman of the board of Fairchild Publications, which publishes the powerful trade paper *Women's Wear Daily.*

Blass and Fairchild are the only famous faces here today. Whereas at Le Cirque or La Grenouille the customers at lunch almost all look as if they'd just stepped out of the society pages, and you can usually be assured of seeing famous faces dotting the dining room, here the patrons look significantly less sophisticated. Of course on another day you might spot Jacqueline Onassis or Richard Nixon or Kathleen Turner or James Levine, conductor of the Metropolitan Opera Orchestra. But you could also very easily be seated next to two older women in sweater vests, women who in other restaurants of this caliber would be relegated to back rooms and even there would look out of place. Here they appear quite comfortable and are clearly quite welcome.

The customers' location in the dining room determines who will be serving them, but unlike most high-end restaurants, which have preferred stations served by preferred captains and waiters, Lutèce rotates the location of its waiters with each meal and the location of its captains weekly. This is done partly to prevent a clubby "in" or "out" feeling, which would result if the regular customers could choose not only their favorite tables but their favorite captains and waiters as well, but mainly because working in the upstairs dining rooms is physically demanding since it involves running up and down the stairs for every course. To avoid exhausting the waiters, a different pair works upstairs at each meal. Since the same partners always work together, they are, like dancers, intimately familiar with each other's rhythm and style.

The tables are divided into three stations: two downstairs and two upstairs. The two stations upstairs share the same captain and busboy. Downstairs, each of the two stations gets its own captain and busboy, as well as its own team of waiters. To encourage teamwork, tips are pooled: the three captains share theirs; the waiters share theirs and give a percentage to the busboys.

Today we will watch one team, captain Luc Chevalier and waiters René Conan and Jean Louis Fontaine, at work. The slight, dapper, brown-haired Luc has been a captain here for nine years and had previously been maître d' at another French restaurant in New York City. René has worked here for more than a decade, and during that time, he and Jean Louis, who has been here for fifteen years, have worked as a team, always with a different captain at every meal. When one of them has the day off, the other floats throughout the restaurant, helping out wherever he is needed. The same holds true for the other pairs of waiters.

Born and raised in France, stocky, blond-haired René came to this country as a young adult and got a job as a busboy at La Grenouille "just to make money." After four months he became a waiter there, a position he held for twelve years. He wasn't very happy there because, he says, referring to Charles Masson, Jr., "he's crazy, that guy. He yells at you for nothing." Indeed, Masson himself once told me that yelling at his workers was a necessary part of doing business and that he wasn't about to "win a popularity contest" with his employees.

René had a friend working at Lutèce, where the atmosphere is significantly more pleasant, and when a waitering job became available, René's friend recommended him for it.

Like their co-workers, Luc, René, and Jean Louis all have only good things to say about working here. "We have a fantastic boss," says the tall, sharp-featured Jean Louis. "He takes care of us. Other restaurants serve good food for the customers and not such great food for the staff. Here the food for the staff is great too. We are like a big family, very all together."

Later, André tells me, "Many say it works like a family. That sounds nice but it's not easy to put it in practice. Sometimes in my position you're not always liked. I have my problems too. Sometimes I'm pretty tough and give them hell but it's over half an hour later. For me it's not difficult to admit I'm wrong when I'm wrong. I'm the kind of guy who can go back and say, 'You're not right but I'm not right either. Let's put it behind us.'

"I try as much as I can so that it works a little like a family. When a guy's with me a year, five years, ten years, you have to have feeling for him a little. I've worked with Jacques since 1955. I have no member of my family with whom I was as long, so of course I like him very much, even though sometimes on work he doesn't do exactly what I want and I tell him and he accepts it and we have no problem. I'm not always pleased with him and he's not always pleased with me. But we have a pretty good rapport. I try to be fair. It doesn't mean that I'm always fair. Nobody's always fair. I work with them, which is a big plus. Many restaurateurs and bosses don't work physically, actually with them. So in many things I am not their boss. I am their co-worker."

For today's lunch, Luc, René, and Jean Louis have been assigned to the eight tables at the rear of the downstairs dining room. Another team has the front eight tables, four in the main dining room and four in the small room where Blass and Fairchild are seated.

Like their counterparts at the other stations, Luc, René, and Jean Louis each have specific duties. As captain, Luc takes the food and wine orders, explaining the selections and making recommendations. His notepad records orders in triplicate: The white originals will go to the kitchen, the yellow copies to the cashier, and the pink copies will stay at the service table.

By reading these slips, the service waiter—in this case René—will know what extra silver and glassware, if any, to put out on a table. Stationed tableside at all times, he will get the glasses and utensils from the nearby service stand. He will also fillet the sole or carve the chicken if necessary.

Jean Louis will bring all the order slips to the kitchen and the bar and carry the food and drinks to the dining room. During the course of the meal, René will keep an eye out for anything the table may need and will judge how slowly or quickly the customers eat. Using this speed as a guide, he will tell Jean Louis when to alert the kitchen to begin preparing the next course.

The timing is based on the dish the table has ordered with the longest cooking time. René and Jean Louis know exactly how long it takes to cook every item served here. For example, they know that a filet mignon takes twelve to fifteen minutes, whereas fish cooks much more quickly. For each table, René must feel out when to tell the kitchen to start cooking.

"Here comes in the professionalism of the waiters," says André. And it does indeed take professionalism to get the timing down correctly. The kitchen staff performs the most stressful and physically demanding duties, but the wait staff's choreography of the meal's presentation and timing is of equal importance and requires a skill of its own.

Watching the captains and waiters work is indeed like watching a choreographed performance. They are constantly on the lookout for what is happening at each of their tables, taking their cues from the customers, spotting for each other like gymnasts. And, whenever they have a few seconds of down time, René and Jean

Louis both stand by the service table and stare at the pink order slips as if they were actors memorizing their lines.

Although the captain takes all the other orders, René takes the initial drink orders. This responsibility falls to the service waiters to ensure that, if a captain is caught up in explaining the food or wine to one table, another table will not be ignored when they sit down. And if Luc and René should both be busy when a third table arrives, then Jean Louis would take that table's drink order.

As this station's first two customers sit down, René takes their drink order and hands it to Jean Louis, who takes it to the bar and waits for Pierre to fill it. Looking up, Pierre notices that a dapper male customer who had been sitting at a table in the bar, waiting for his lunch date to arrive, has disappeared. "Where'd that smelly guy go?" he asks Mirielle.

"What smelly guy?" she says, glancing at Simone, as if expecting a reprimand. None is forthcoming.

"The one wearing Chanel."

"I didn't notice." (The "smelly guy" had gone to the bathroom.)

Another male customer arrives and kisses Simone hello on the cheek. She doesn't look too happy about it but lets him do it. "He has a house in the Hamptons," Pierre says as Simone takes the customer into the dining room.

Simone returns and answers the ringing telephone. It is a customer calling to say he will be late. "No problem," she says in her French accent. "You will be welcome." She speaks in a melodic, coquettish voice that is at odds with her somewhat matronly appearance.

Returning to the dining room with the drinks, Jean Louis hands them to René, who puts them on the table, and Luc hands the couple two menus. The busboy has poured water automatically, as he will do for all the tables.

Had the customers put the menus down on the table and continued their conversation, Luc would have walked away, returning to describe the specials when they picked up their menus again. But since they looked at their menus right away, Luc describes the lunch specials to them and then leaves them to peruse the menu.

The lunch menu is a large, laminated, single-sided sheet with a slot in its center, and every day the captains insert a handwritten description of the plat du jour into this slot. Today it says escalope of veal. A special appetizer, pastry stuffed with crab and scallops, is also available but does not appear on the menu.

Lunch is price-fixed at thirty-eight dollars, and for that amount you choose an appetizer, an entrée, and dessert. Having a price-fixed menu, according to André, is the best way for a restaurant to guarantee a steady profit. During its first fifteen years, Lutèce's offerings were priced à la carte. As the restaurant rose in fame, says André, "more and more people came here just so they could say they did.

"They would have a salad, a small main course, and they wouldn't eat dessert," he continues. "They didn't eat more than twenty or twenty-five dollars' worth of food [at dinner], and they took up space that could have been for a person who would have spent more. And that's why we became price-fixed. We are a small operation and have to make a certain amount of money on each of our seats in order to exist. Whatever people eat, we still have the same overhead, the same staff to pay."

Like lunch, dinner is also price-fixed, at sixty dollars. "In France the price of lunch and dinner is the same," says André. "In American culture people can't understand why lunch would be the same price as dinner. We have to adapt to this kind of thinking because we are doing business here. For lunch we have to design a menu that costs less. We don't cut in quality but we offer different things." Basically, lunch is lighter and its ingredients aren't as pricey.

"People say we are too expensive," says André. "I don't think that's true. If you go to a restaurant of our caliber and have four people for dinner you'll spend five hundred dollars.

"The press has brainwashed the public into this new trend of bistros," he continues, referring to the slew of articles that have appeared on the trend toward lower-priced restaurants. "How can I serve two for dinner for eighty dollars? A good piece of meat costs twenty dollars minimum, not counting wild mushrooms or whatever else I serve with it. People get much more effort for their money here. If you come in for dinner and you feel like having chicken, it costs me a dollar and some a pound. But if your husband feels like medallions of veal, that costs me ten times more. But you and your husband pay the same. You both pay sixty dollars. On one thing I make more and on another I make less. The person who comes in and eats pea soup pays the same thing as the one who eats marinated salmon but the marinated salmon costs me much more than the soup."

Ideally, André would like to do away with a menu completely but, he says, "you need one because if people have never been here, they sit down and they expect that you give them one. But it's the specials that we serve the most. I like to say 'Today I'd like to cook this for you.' That's the excitement of having a restaurant. The customers who know us don't bother to look at the menu.

"When a chef makes a menu he has to consider everything," André continues. "To write a menu is one thing but to be able to furnish it is another." In planning a menu, restaurants have to think about how they would be able to fill orders under the worst conditions, if all the customers came and ordered at once. To cover this possibility, they offer some dishes that are grilled, some that are sautéed, and some that are roasted, so that the space in the kitchen can be used intelligently.

And, André says, "if you go with too many complicated things, then your people are not able to produce it fast enough. That happens in some restaurants who are not one hundred percent professional. You have your appetizer and then you wait two hours before you get your main course. Why? Because they don't have the physical time to prepare it, and why is that so? Because the chef didn't have enough experience or common sense to design his menu according to the strength of his staff. If service is slow, many times it's the kitchen that is not able to send it out. I am very strict on that. I am very on-the-ball."

The fare changes rarely—only when the existing menus start to look dog-eared and need to be replaced. "That's an opportunity for us to put a few new dishes on," says André. "But not too much changes because that's the basic menu, and it's the specials that are changing all the time." What does change seasonally is the key ingredients or garnishes used for menu items. For example, in the spring baby chicken may be served with cepes and in the fall with morels. In the spring the sweetbreads may be served with capers instead of mushrooms, or the duck with raspberries instead of pears or apples.

"But basically," André says, "you need those things on the menu. You need a chicken, you need a sweetbread because that's what people expect. That doesn't change but you change the way it's done a little bit."

Some of the dishes on the menu have been there since the day Lutèce first opened its doors. These include the creamed pea soup, the individual beef Wellingtons, and the snails in tiny terrines served with shallots and garlic butter. The salmon *en croûte* has been an offering since 1965. Although some food critics, like *New York* magazine's Gael Greene and *New York Newsday*'s Jane Freiman, turn up their noses at this lack of innovation, these items continue to be popular.

As if to illustrate this point, the woman at René's table orders the pea soup and the man orders escargot. They both order the plat du jour as their entrée.

Luc asks if they would like any wine but they say no. Had they said yes, René would have put out the appropriate glasses for red or white wine. Seeing Luc retrieve the menus and walk away, the busboy puts bread and butter on the table.

Neither René nor Jean Louis heard what the couple ordered, yet by looking at the pink copy of the order form, each will know what to do, when to do it, and who ordered which dish. This is because Luc writes the orders in a consistent manner. Although he takes women's orders first and the host's last, he always writes the dishes according to seat number. As Luc stands facing the table, the person on his left gets assigned the number one, and the numbers go clockwise around the table.

The kitchen, too, takes some of its cues from the way the order is written. Normally, the cooks begin work on the appetizers as soon as the slip arrives in the kitchen. But if this couple had wanted to linger over their drinks before eating, the captain would have written a large *X* on top of the order form. This would have told the kitchen to wait about ten minutes.

Luc leaves the pink order slip on the service table and hands the two other copies to Jean Louis, who brings one to the kitchen and one to the cashier. René, looking at the order on the service table, and seeing that the couple ordered a soup and a fish appetizer, lays out the appropriate silverware.

In the kitchen, the soup just needs to be ladled out of its hot canister and the escargot take only minutes to bake. In no time at all, Jean Louis returns with the food and René serves it to the customers.

As René places the dishes on the table, the man says he's changed his mind and that he would like to order a bottle of wine. René takes the order, even though this is officially Luc's responsibility. "You never tell the customer to wait for the captain," René tells me. He writes the wine order on a slip of white paper and hands it to Jean Louis, who fetches the bottle of wine. René, in the meantime, crosses the appetizers off the couple's pink order slip. This is done to remind himself and Jean Louis that the couple has already been served the appetizer. When the entrée is served, it will similarly be crossed off.

This will prevent a mistake like one that occurred when some friends and I dined at Webb City in Sag Harbor, Long Island. After our coffee and dessert plates were cleared, our embarrassed and overwhelmed young waitress sent a busboy over to ask if we'd been served our entrées. She couldn't remember if she'd given them to us or not.

Keeping to the right, as in traffic, Simone leads another elderly couple to their table. As she walks, she scans the dining room to make sure all is well. She is ever vigilant, every so often scolding a captain for loudly scraping a table leg against the floor as he pulled it out for a customer, or shooing a busboy out of a customer's way with a barely perceptible wave of her hand; she even scolded me once for opening the kitchen door without checking the hallway first and bumping the door into a customer. Simone's scoldings are not verbal—they are delivered via soft shrieks of disapproval, a glare, and a quick shake of her head. If it happens once, believe me, you don't want it to happen again.

The couple arrive at their table and the man heads for the seat facing the dining room, the seat traditionally meant for women. Simone stops him by saying, "You will be more comfortable here." Listening to her, he sits facing the wall.

René takes their drink orders, and as Jean Louis goes for the drinks, Luc hands the couple a set of menus. They put them down on the table and so Luc retreats. He will return to describe the specials when the couple pick up their menus, again a sign that they are ready to consider what they would like to eat.

As Simone returns to the dining room with a group of three men, René clears the soup and appetizer plates from the first table and hands the plates to the busboy. The busboy carries the plates to the kitchen, where he passes them in through a small waist-high window cut into the wall next to the dishwasher.

Luc notices that the second couple have picked up their menus and so he goes over to describe the specials.

André, in the meantime, heads upstairs to take the order of Elwyn D. Lieberman, president of the paper supplier Allan and Gray Corporation, who eats here once a week. I'd met him on an earlier visit, and when I asked him what brought him back again and again, he said, "I told André no salt in my food and he never forgets. Coffee you can get in a demitasse cup or a regular one. I don't like demitasse cups because I have large hands. He will never forget that my coffee is served in a big cup."

"That's our work," André tells me later. "We have to remember. That's the difference between a restaurant run by the owner and a restaurant that is corporate. I know him for a long time, so right away it pops into my head: no salt, big cup.

"Most of the time I take his order and right away I write, 'No salt,' and I tell the busboys, 'Hey, remember. A big cup.' But most of the captains and waiters remember these things, too."

André asks Lieberman and his guest what they feel like eating today and the woman says she would like something light. "I could make you crab and scallops in a pastry," says André. "It's not the lightest in the world. We go lighter elsewhere."

To Lieberman André says, "It's a little salty," and the man picks asparagus instead.

André writes this down and then, to the woman, says, "For the main course if you want fish I do fresh salmon. It's smoked a little bit and then roasted in the skin. It's served on salad. Or you could have a chicken dish or fillet of sole." Both of them order the salmon.

André drops off this order in the kitchen and then goes into the downstairs garden room to take the order of the three men Simone has seated, one of whom is a regular customer.

"I'm on a diet," this customer says by way of greeting.

"We have roasted salmon. We smoke it a little bit as an appetizer."

"Okay. Whatever you say."

"Then for a main course I can make for you fish or also chicken."

André looks at a second man at the table. "Are you on a diet too?"

"I am now," he jokes.

"Did you see the recent articles saying how you can eat what you wish if you have red wine with it?" the third man says.

"Oh, good," says the second. Nonetheless, all three men order the roasted salmon as their appetizer and roasted baby chickens as their entrée.

"Do you want sauce?" André says.

"A drop," the regular patron answers. "We don't want to hurt your feelings."

André walks into the kitchen and calls out, "Three small *saumon rôti* and put three *poussin* in the oven." He posts the order near all the others that have come into the kitchen and Jacques puts the three chickens in the oven right away since they take a long time to cook.

"Yes, sir," Henry says, acknowledging that he heard the salmon order. Then he looks at the neighboring order slip and says, "Mr. Lieberman."

"No salt," says André. Henry nods and André heads back out into the dining room. He walks up to another table and one of the customers says, "What do you have to eat?"

"What do you like? What do you feel like having?"

"What's good today?" the man asks.

"Everything," says the man's companion.

"I don't want to say that," André says, smiling.

Back in the kitchen Henry is talking through the window to a friend of his who has come to lunch with his family. The friend gives Henry an anti–George Bush T-shirt, and after the friend is seated, Henry says, with obvious affection for his friend of twenty years, "The Chef's customers bring him money. This is what my customers bring me."

André had noticed that Henry was talking to this young man and asks, "Is he a friend of yours?"

Henry nods. André asks for his friend's name and goes out to take the family of four's order. While there exists an unspoken understanding between André and the regulars that they will put themselves in André's hands and that, to them, he will say the very special words, "Today, I can make for you . . ." André treats people he doesn't know in a more traditional way.

"Did anyone explain to you the specials?" he asks Henry's friends. When they say no he tells them what they are. "Today we have *chaussons,* pastry filled with crab and scallops, or we have salmon, smoked a little bit and then roasted and served on a salad. And veal escalope, this is veal in cheese and bread crumbs, sautéed."

All four order the salmon and the veal. Back in the kitchen André asks Henry if he put any salmon aside for his friend's table. Henry shakes his head no, and André goes downstairs to see how much salmon is left. Luckily, there's just enough for that table's order.

"Do you have time to smoke another salmon for dinner if I order one now?" André asks Bill.

Bill nods and so André calls Phil Rozzo and asks, "How fast can I get a salmon? Six pounds in fillet."

Rozzo tells him it will be at Lutèce within the hour and André says, "Great. Send them."

On the way back upstairs he tells me that he has a customer coming tonight who always asks if roasted salmon is available. "He doesn't always order it but he always asks and so I want to have it," André says.

The couple at the second table have finished their appetizers. Seeing this, Jean Louis goes to the kitchen, and, through the long window across from the stove, he calls in the table number and tells the cooks that the couple are ready for their entrées. He then returns to the dining room, where he puts an *X* in the bottom-right corner of that table's order slip on the service cart. That *X* is a reminder to himself that he told the kitchen to start cooking the main course. After the main course has been served, Jean Louis will cross off the items and place the order slip under the linen on the service cart, so that he, René, and Luc will know that the couple will soon be ready to order dessert. The dessert order is written on a separate piece of paper, and after he takes it, the captain will put that order on the service cart. René will remove the first slip, the one listing the appetizers and entrées, from the service cart, making sure the wine order has been written on the bottom of the slip. If no wine was ordered, then the words "no wine" have to appear. These slips will be brought down to the cashier later.

After the customers have finished their entrées, the busboy or René will clear the table and the busboy will pass a cleaning utensil over it to get the crumbs off. Luc will take the dessert order and hand that order to Jean Louis, who will bring one copy to the kitchen and one to the cashier. The cashier will also get a list of what the customers at that table had to drink and, while they are having dessert, will prepare their computerized checks.

The plates won't be taken from the table until everyone is finished eating. When people ask Luc for the check, it is René's responsibility to get it. Seeing that Luc has asked the first couple who sat down if they wanted anything else and that they have said no, René walks downstairs and gets their check even before the customers ask for it. "This way it will be ready when they do," he says. "We try to anticipate whatever we can."

As I watch the captains and waiters work, I notice that they use the word "you" a lot. As Jeffrey Steingarten reported in *Vogue,* several students at the Professional Service School tried an experiment at the restaurants where they worked. "They inserted the words *for you* into every sentence," Steingarten wrote, "even when it sounded silly, as in 'I'd be happy to get a fresh cup of coffee for you,' or 'Is this steak done all right for you?' Their tips increased by twenty percent."

The captains also say "for you" or "you" frequently. "What would please you as a main course?" they ask. "Do you wish to have a salad or fresh asparagus?"

The latter question is slightly tricky since it sounds as if those items are included in the price of the meal. They aren't. At dinner there is a supplemental charge of $4.50 for the first and $5.00 for the second. For a table of four, the latter would add $20.00 to the tab.

Offering the customers a choice of two items—rather than just saying, "Would you like a salad?"—is also a savvy food-service technique. The textbook *Professional Table Service* instructs waiters and captains-to-be always to offer customers alternatives. When you ask a customer if he or she wants to try one dish, you "allow the guest to respond negatively," says the book. "If you add to your recommendation a second choice, your chances for a successful sale are much better."

Besides "for you," the waiters and captains also frequently say "we," as in "What else would we like?" The "we" is a nice inclusive touch, emphasizing that the service staff and patrons are linked in this enjoyable experience.

"Here we are," says René as he puts fillets of sole in front of a customer. "That's for you."

André walks through the restaurant to take another table's order. His presence causes the conversation at many of the tables to turn to the restaurant. A young couple, with what looks like a set of parents, regale the elder couple with a limited biography of André. They are obviously thrilled to be not only in his restaurant but in his presence.

Among the customers I spoke with over the course of my time at Lutèce, most had only good things to say about it. Only a few expressed any doubts. One couple—Dr. Norman Juskowitz and his wife, Ruth—questioned why they were able to get a reservation so easily. It was Ruth's birthday, and she chose Lutèce at the last minute because "it's a quality place without being high-toned. It's soft and they make you feel welcome and not minimal."

But, she said, "we called yesterday and there was no problem to get a reservation. Why not?"

Hearing this, I was reminded of the games Charles Masson, Jr., played at La Grenouille and I realized that he had a point. People really do seem to want what they can't get. They *want* a restaurant to be a hard place to get into.

Some of the people I met seemed to *look* for negatives. For instance, on one occasion, eight women were here celebrating their friend's fiftieth birthday. One of them asked if I was "writing good things about this restaurant."

"I'm writing whatever I see and hear," I said. "Why? Do you know of any bad things?"

"Yes," she said. "I was here for my birthday a few years ago with my husband and I wanted duck but they told us you could only get duck for two. My husband didn't want it. So we looked at the menu again and decided to get the duck after all. When we ordered it they were out of it." She stops and gives me a significant look, as if she had just told me that the captain cut her fingers off at the table.

"Well, that happens," I said.

"So *then,*" she continued, "they suggested we order chicken since that was the closest thing to duck. They said it was really good. So we ordered it and they brought us five chicken wings. *Chicken wings.*" She gave me a significant look again, and when I didn't react, she said, "Although the sauce was really great. It was one of the best sauces I've ever had."

One of the woman's friends commented, "You know, that really isn't such a bad story."

Listening to this woman, I was reminded of an earlier conversation with André in which he'd talked about customers who come looking for trouble, looking for things to be wrong. This woman seemed to be such a customer, but in the end, even she begrudgingly agreed that she had enjoyed her most recent meal here.

When I repeated her negative comments to André, he shrugged and said that, yes, he would serve chicken wings, but only at lunch and with something special, like sweetbreads and wild mushrooms. Then, looking at me for a long moment, he finally said, with no sarcasm but with a slight twinkle in his eyes: "Ask her only one thing. Why did she come back?"

$\mathscr{R}$ACK OF LAMB PERSILLÉ

FOR 2 PEOPLE

1 rack of lamb (about
  1¼ lb.)
1 Tb oil
Salt, pepper
1 Tb Dijon mustard
½ cup fresh bread
  crumbs

3 tsp chopped parsley
1 small clove of garlic,
  minced
⅛ tsp thyme
2 tsp melted butter

Brush the rack of lamb with oil and season with salt and pepper. Roast in a 400-degree oven for 12 minutes. Brush mustard on the meat.

Mix bread crumbs, parsley, garlic, thyme, and melted butter. Spread this mixture on top of the rack.

Continue roasting for 15 minutes.

Let rack rest for 10 minutes before carving.

2:00 P.M.

*A*t this hour, the tables are all full, the orders have all been taken, and lunch service begins to wind down. While lunch was being served upstairs, preparations for tonight's dinner and tomorrow's lunch were under way downstairs.

At noon, twenty-four-year-old Stuart Alpert arrived and began work in the prep kitchen. Tall and skinny, with a pointy nose, angular features, and wire-frame glasses, Stuart is the assistant cook responsible for butchering the bulk of the meat as well as working at the *garde manger* station for the last part of lunch and all of dinner.

After asking his co-workers if they'd seen *The Odd Couple* last night—a show Stuart watches religiously—Stuart confronted the pile of meat stacked up on the counter just inside the entrance to the prep kitchen. Just by glancing at the pile, he could tell how busy the day before had been—the higher the pile, the busier the day, since more meat needed to be reordered. Today's pile is considered medium-size. Because of the profit-sharing policy, everyone in the kitchen takes consistent note of the volume of business.

But no matter how much business was done yesterday, and how much meat was delivered today, Stuart has from noon until two o'clock to butcher all of it. Stuart, with the frequently hyper energy of youth, works fast even when speed isn't necessary. He prides himself on being able to butcher a loin of veal in seven minutes, "but that's reckless," he says. He and Joe, who are good friends, once raced to see who could butcher a loin of veal faster, and Stuart won by a long shot.

Stuart likes to talk, and today, as he sliced a loin of veal into its component cuts, he talked about his parents; the spread of Lyme disease in his parents' Westchester neighborhood; his New York City roommate; his girlfriend; the genesis of his friendship with Joe; and his decision to pursue cooking as a profession.

Stuart is the son of a stockbroker father and an artist mother, and he knew he wanted to cook for a living ever since he was eleven years old. "I went to an auto show and was more interested in watching the guy making crepes than in looking at the cars."

Cooking wasn't the career his parents had hoped he would pursue. "I was supposed to be a stockbroker just like my dad, or I could have been an artist like my mother. I had a choice between *A* and *B*." After a year and a half of business school he chose *C*.

He graduated from the French Culinary Institute in Manhattan, briefly worked at the Terrace Restaurant on New York's Upper West Side, and then signed on for a two-year apprenticeship at L'Hostellerie Bressane in upstate New York, where he met Joe. Afterward, he came to Lutèce.

"Long term," Stuart said, "I would definitely like to have my own place. The 'when' is at least eight years from now. So many restaurants go down. I think in New York there's a fifty percent failure rate in the first six months. That happens when the guy has no idea of what he's doing. I'm too young to worry about all that stuff. I would rather cook and enjoy it now."

The thing that surprised him most about working as a cook, he said, is "the incredible amount of pressure."

"My brother works on the floor of the American Stock Exchange and my dad is in a trading room. I knew that was all about pressure and ulcers but I didn't expect cooking to be as high-pressure as it is. People who are having a mid-life crisis and want to change what they're doing say to me, 'I want to cook,' and I say, 'Don't do it unless you love to cook. Don't just do it because you dislike what you're already doing.' "

Talking all the while, Stuart kept his attention focused on his work, slicing, pulling, and tugging. All of the cooks here have their own knives, which they choose primarily by how the knives fit in their hands, and which they sharpen every day. Stuart's razor-sharp Hoffritz knife cut through the meat easily.

As I watched, the meat began to resemble artists' clay, mostly because of the quick and efficient way he pulled, tugged, and rolled the bloodless stuff in his hands. He lined up the different cuts—tenderloins, loins, chops, flank—on the counter where Joe had worked this morning. (Joe had since moved over to work at Bill's counter.)

As he worked, Stuart discarded the fat into a large plastic-lined garbage can and threw the bones into a large white plastic bucket. Jacques will roast them this afternoon and they will simmer overnight to make veal stock. Stuart placed leftover scraps of meat in a smaller bucket. These will be used for staff meals.

"We eat so many veal scraps here," Bill once told me, "that when I go out to eat I never order veal. I'm sick of it. The same goes for dessert. I never have it because it's here. I live in it. It's sickening after a while."

As he cut the fat from a second loin of veal, Stuart said, "The French are meticulous about not wasting anything. Even the fat is sometimes used. The chef mixes it with bird seed and puts it out for the birds at his country house.

"They like their houses and take the time to do things like work in the garden," he said, referring to André and Bill. "Billy brings home eggshells. If you crush them and put them in the soil, it draws out the vitamins or something. Or else you put them in water and then you water your plants with it. I don't have a garden, but if I did I wouldn't spend my weekend crawling around on my hands and knees in it getting mud in my face. I'd be inside watching the game."

As he cut off a huge piece of fat, Stuart, who is keenly aware of how much things cost, said, unasked, "The whole loin is probably a hundred and twenty or a hundred and thirty dollars. They sell it by weight, and that includes the fat and the kidneys. You're paying for veal and you get a lot of waste. We usually send the kidneys back." When I expressed surprise at this fact, he said, "Would you eat a urine filter? For my money I'd rather have a hamburger."

After he finished butchering the veal, Stuart turned to the beef and lamb, wrapping all the cuts destined for customer consumption in plastic wrap and putting them in their respective places on the right side of the walk-in refrigerator. He placed the fresh meat under the meat already in the refrigerator so that the older meat would get used first.

As he wiped his hands on a clean white towel, he said, "Seventeen cents a towel." This is the laundering fee for each one. "Imagine that. Three hundred towels a day at seventeen cents."

Then, referring to the menu he said, "Everything costs extra." (This really isn't true, although there are supplemental charges for the vegetables and a few other items.) "That's how you stay in business. If you order asparagus, it's five dollars extra; salad is four dollars and fifty cents extra; caviar is fifty-eight dollars extra. That's . . . let me see . . . thirteen Big Macs. That would be thirteen dinners for this kid. I'm not about to spend that kind of money for caviar."

In fact, it seems he's not about to spend any kind of money on food. Besides getting free meals, Stuart is perpetually snacking. Finished butchering the meat, he took a terrine out of the refrigerator, cut a thin slice, and cut this slice in half again. He kept one half for himself and gave the other to Joe, saying, "Half and half, fifty-fifty." Joe smiled as he accepted the terrine.

"We have this tradition," said Stuart. "We split everything." The tradition started when they were apprentices at L'Hostellerie Bressane. "There was another cook there who never showed up for work one day and left a drawer full of knives behind him," said Stuart. "We split the knives fifty-fifty."

Fortified by his snack, Stuart took out a white plastic container filled with the Boston lettuce Bernardo had washed earlier this morning. Leaf by leaf, he removed the stems, throwing these into another white bucket. The stems will be served to the staff along with any slightly wilted or brown leftover lettuce.

He left a few big leaves whole (these will be used as garnishes for the serving platters) and tore the smaller ones into bite-size pieces for the customers' salads.

Ramon walked by, pausing to slap Stuart on the back. He tried to make it seem like nothing more than a fraternal slap but Stuart knew right away something was up. "What'd he put on my back?" he asked me.

"It's a sticker saying 'Association of Chilean Salmon Farmers.' " I peeled the sticker off. As I handed it to Stuart, he rolled his eyes and looked around for Ramon.

But before Stuart could say anything, Ramon returned from the outer room yelling at him. Although he was speaking English I didn't understand a word except the last, in Spanish—"Stupido."

"Did you get that, Stuart?" said Bill.

Stuart nodded, wiped his hands on a fresh towel (seventeen cents), and walked into the small room. After I asked what Ramon had said, Stuart pointed at the two trays of asparagus sitting across from the oven and, imitating Ramon's booming voice and his accent, repeated Ramon's words, "If you need the oven, you go take the oven, because at five o'clock your asparagoo is going to sit outside, you stupido."

"From the time he's finished [peeling] the asparagus he keeps yelling all day for us to put it in. 'Asparagoo! Asparagoo!' " Stuart cried, imitating Ramon's pronunciation.

Stuart put the trays of asparagus in the combi oven, which, besides roasting, can also steam foods. As the steam enveloped the asparagus, Stuart shoveled ice out of the big ice machine into a deep metal tray. The asparagus will be placed on this ice when it's cooked. Stuart glanced toward the oven again and said, "That oven is really good. Lord knows how much that thing cost."

Back in the other room, everyone was silently performing his individual duties. Bill was stuffing the saddles of lamb for tomorrow's lunch. Joe was making candied grapefruit rinds. Ramon was working on the complimentary cookies that are always offered to each table. Bernardo, who had returned from a trip up the block to inspect that morning's laundry delivery, was making a small batch of candies that the captains will also present, along with Joe's candied grapefruit rinds, to each table at the end of dinner service.

At one o'clock Guido headed for the upstairs kitchen and joined the man who was washing pots and dishes there. From noon to one it's slow enough for one man to handle the volume of dishes, but after one o'clock he needs help.

As two o'clock approached, it was Stuart's turn to leave for the upstairs kitchen, where he relieved Juan at the *garde manger* station. Juan then came down here to work on the pastry-wrapped baby quail for tonight's dinner party. Before leaving, Stuart grabbed a handful of chocolate pieces from a bag on the shelf over Bill's counter and handed Joe half, saying, "Half and half, right down the middle."

He then took a fresh paper *toque* from a pile on a shelf and cut it down to the same height as those everyone else had on upstairs. Placing it on his head, he made for the stairs.

As he approached the kitchen door, he focused on the metal spike positioned on the ledge inside the door window. If lots of little white slips had been impaled on it, that would mean Stuart had a lot of dessert orders awaiting him. But since the metal spike was bare, he knew he could relax slightly.

As he walked into the kitchen, his eyes darted almost imperceptibly to the small monthly calendar taped on the wall by the door to see if the tiny little square with today's date had anything written on it. Occasions commemorated on this calendar include co-workers' birthdays, legal holidays, and personal milestones. For example, one square had a penciled notation reading "MDH." This stands for "miracles do happen." "That's the day Joe actually paid me back some money he owed me," Stuart said. Today's square, however, is blank.

Since no dessert orders await him, Stuart gets to work taking inventory of his station, seeing what he'll have to bring up from the downstairs kitchen.

The waiters in the meantime are accepting payment from the customers and running credit cards through the credit-card machines. They stick around until the last customers in their station leave, and then they go on their break. With two or two and a half hours to kill, they run personal errands or go to a nearby park to read the paper. René and a few others frequently go to OTB.

With the end of the meal approaching, André makes his usual rounds through the dining rooms, asking if people were satisfied with their meals. Finished with their work in the kitchen, Jacques and Henry head down to the prep kitchen, where Jacques will chop vegetables for tomorrow's sauces and soups and Henry will prepare any special sauces and garnishes needed for the fish dishes he will be cooking at dinner.

The prep kitchen is now crowded, with all of the morning workers as well as George Troisgros, son of the late three-star French chef Jean Troisgros, who arrived for work at two. George, who has dark hair, a beard, and striking light green eyes with a darker green rim, is as reserved as Stuart is sociable. In fact, Stuart once told me that when he first began working at Lutèce, he noticed that few of the others talked to George. "They told me not to talk to George, that he likes to work by himself in the corner," says Stuart. "But it wasn't true. No one talked to George because everyone thought you weren't supposed to talk to him. He's a nice guy."

He may be a nice guy but he's a private one, and his response to my questions about his background comes hard. Part of the reason for this is because English is difficult for him. As he speaks—in a very heavy French accent—he frequently has to stop to think of the English word for what he is trying to say. But soon the story comes together.

Born in France, George began his apprenticeship with his famous father and uncle at their restaurant, Les Frères Troisgros. "We lived above the restaurant so we were always at the restaurant," he says. "I was pushed a little bit to go into the business but then I started to like it."

For one and a half years he cleaned and chopped vegetables at the family restaurant. He finished the second half of his apprenticeship at the three-star Auberge de l'Ill in Illhaeusern, one of the most renowned restaurants in France. Like most apprentices, George changed stations every few months, so that by the end he had learned to do everything.

After receiving his professional certification in 1974, he went into the army for a year and then went to work at Louis Outhier in Cannes for the March-to-October 1975 season. He started by prepping the fish, then moved up to cooking it.

In October he went to Paris, where he worked at the famous Lasserre for two years, then moved to Régine's, where he worked for a few months with Michel Guérard, the three-star French chef who invented "cuisine minceur," a school of low-calorie French cooking, and who today runs Eugénie-les-Bains, a luxurious country inn and spa in southwestern France. When Guérard was named chef/consultant for Régine's in New York City, George came with him.

He worked with Guérard for fourteen months, then moved to Le Relais on Madison Avenue. He came to Lutèce eleven years ago to work in the position he holds today.

George got this job through his father, whom André met in 1965. On his way to Alsace, André had stopped to eat at Paul Bocuse's restaurant in Lyons. It was the first time he met Paul Bocuse, who said, "You have to meet Troisgros while you're here." André made the detour to Troisgros' village and had dinner at the restaurant. "After dinner he and his wife joined us and we were blah blah blah until one in the morning," recalls André, who enjoyed not only Troisgros' personality but also his cooking. He asked for the recipe for duckling with juniper berries, which remains on Lutèce's menu to this day.

George, who cooks all the meat and poultry dishes during dinner service, begins his workday by slicing some of Stuart's larger cuts of meat into smaller ones, trimming the last vestiges of fat from them. He also does the final preparation of the garnishes that will be served with the dishes he cooks. He quickly peels and chops carrots, onions, and turnips, which will be combined and used as the garnish for the poultry.

That done, he puts some mushrooms and meat on a tray and carries them upstairs. Seeing George, Stuart whips off his toque, since George's appearance means lunch service is officially over and dinner preparations have begun in earnest. Simone now makes her way upstairs to the Soltners' apartment; she won't be seen again until the start of dinner service.

Denis Fitzgerald has remained in the upstairs kitchen with Stuart. A 1984 graduate of the Culinary Institute of America, Denis worked at the River Café in Brooklyn for two years and then came here. At both lunch and dinner he is responsible for ladling out the soups, cooking the hot appetizers, and sautéing the noodles and vegetables. Besides this, he makes dinner for André and Simone and, separately, dinner for the staff. He now begins making the latter meal.

George works at the stove that, until now, has been Jacques's domain. As George puts the meats and mushrooms in the refrigerator across from his stove, Denis, who is working on the same side of the kitchen as George, says, "Tell her about your daughter." He is referring to George's baby girl, born in the beginning of 1991. Offended by this personal revelation, George winces. He doesn't tell me about his daughter but he does say to Denis, "I forgot the picture, Denis, I'm sorry."

As George sets up his station, Stuart pulls out the little white buckets of salad ingredients and dessert sauces from the three refrigerators under his counter. He consolidates some of the contents and dumps everything into separate, clean, white containers. He gives the old containers to the potwasher, saying, *"Más tarde,"* which means "later" in Spanish. This means these containers are not a priority for him to wash. The potwasher grumbles and Stuart says, "I always put everything into clean containers out of habit. I guess if I was the potwasher I'd get a little tense too."

Stuart's refrigerators hold an assortment of cold desserts, like *crème au caramel,* crepes and crepe batter, milk, cream, and dessert sauces, as well as pâtés, terrines, and salads.

Stuart smells some containers, tastes the contents of a few others. "I organize the station exactly the way I want it so that I know where everything is," he says as he works.

After wiping down the refrigerator shelves and putting everything back in its place, Stuart checks the liquor and other supplies he'll need for cooking soufflés tonight—Grand Marnier concentrate and rum, Sanka granules for mocha soufflés, and cocoa powder for the chocolate ones.

He plugs in the two-burner hot plate he has taken from a shelf over his counter. The left burner is for warming the sauce served with the soufflés. The right burner is for boiling the hot salted water into which the asparagus will be dropped just before being served.

The hot plate in place, Stuart puts some sugar into a small pot on the stove. Waiting for it to melt, he pulls out the plastic buckets filled with various bite-size greens and mixes the greens in a big bowl. He removes some slightly brown leaves, saying, "And this is for the fellas," meaning the staff.

When the sugar is ready, Stuart takes Bernardo's candies and puts one on each end of a wooden skewer. He spreads a clean white towel on the counter (seventeen cents) and places a box of aluminum foil on top of it. After dipping the candies into the sugar, he rests the skewers across the width of the box and leaves them there while the candy pieces cool off and harden. Stuart places gold paper doilies on two plates, saying, "We reuse doilies as much as possible. If they don't look like they've been walked on, we save them." Once the candies are cool he takes them off the skewers and arranges them on the two plates.

Next, he goes back downstairs to bring up additional supplies: candied grapefruit rinds, pâté, raspberry soufflés, ice cream, salads, and artichokes.

Downstairs, Ramon is taking a tray of cookies out of the oven. Stuart grabs one, breaks it in two, and hands one half to Joe.

After carrying his provisions upstairs, Stuart begins a dizzying series of chores, executing them with extraordinary speed and efficiency. First, he pours vinaigrette into a bowl, and pours the liquidy mushroom-tomato stuffing, which will be served inside the artichokes, into a white plastic container.

Next he puts pastry cream that George made yesterday into a Kitchen Aid blender and whips it together with egg yolks. This cream is the basis of the dessert soufflés.

Then, as George checks in a bread delivery from the Tom Cat Bakery, Stuart pulls down the soufflé molds and butters them. Seeing what Stuart is doing, George asks him if there is enough pastry cream. Stuart says yes, there is another container of it in the refrigerator.

Finished with the molds, Stuart wants to scallop the edges of a few lemon halves that will garnish some of the fish dishes but he can't find his serrated knife. "Where's killer?" he says to Denis. He calls the small, sharp knife "killer" because everyone who uses it cuts himself. Denis spots the knife on the counter and hands it to Stuart.

After finishing the lemons, Stuart fills a few waxed-paper cones with cream. These cones will be used for writing either "Lutèce" or a special inscription on the soufflés.

He will spend the rest of the afternoon attending to a myriad of details, such as beating the cream for a dessert of puff pastry, fruit, and cream, refilling creamers with milk and a few with heavy cream, and removing the waxed-paper collars on the raspberry soufflés.

Downstairs in the prep kitchen, Jacques, Juan, and Henry continue working alongside the morning crew. Jacques is preparing the soups; Juan is wrapping the baby quail in puff pastry for to-night's party; Henry is preparing the saffron sauce for a fish special for dinner. Exiting the refrigerator, Henry asks Jacques to order some red and yellow peppers for tomorrow.

André walks downstairs to see if anyone in the prep kitchen has any questions for him. They don't. André looks around, notes what everyone is doing, and then, satisfied that all is progressing well, walks back upstairs. He pours himself another black iced coffee and makes his way toward the staircase leading to his third-floor office.

$\mathscr{G}$OUJONNETTES OF BASS

FOR 4 PEOPLE

1½ lbs. skinless fillet of
   bass
½ cup flour mixed with
   1 cup fresh bread
   crumbs

2 Tb peanut oil
1 Tb sweet butter
Salt, pepper
1 Tb chopped parsley

Prepare coulis of fresh tomatoes (recipe below).

Cut the fillet of bass into pieces about 2½ inches long. Roll the pieces in the flour and bread crumbs.

Place 2 tablespoons of oil and 1 tablespoon of butter in a large skillet. When hot, add the fish in one layer. Sauté for about 5 minutes over high heat until nicely browned. Add salt and pepper.

Place fish in center of 4 hot plates. Pour coulis of tomatoes around. Sprinkle with parsley.

Serve hot.

$\mathscr{C}$OULIS OF FRESH TOMATOES

3 Tb olive oil
1 shallot, finely chopped
1 lb. fresh ripe tomatoes
   (peeled and seeded)
   cut in small pieces
1 tsp tomato paste

1 clove garlic
1 scant tsp sugar
1 small bouquet garni
Salt, pepper
½ cup chicken stock

Heat oil in heavy saucepan. Add shallot. Cook slowly over medium heat for 2 minutes.

Add tomatoes, tomato paste, garlic, sugar, bouquet garni, salt, pepper, and chicken stock. Bring to a boil. Cover and cook for 20 minutes, stirring occasionally.

Discard bouquet garni. Transfer tomato mixture to a blender and puree until smooth.

3:00 P.M.

On his way upstairs André hears the doorbell ring. The front door is always locked during off hours and André now opens it to a young male chef who has arranged to drop off his résumé at this time.

"We don't have anything available right now but I wanted to meet you anyway," says André, who always agrees to meet briefly anyone interested in working for him. "It helps to see the face. Then when something does come up I will remember you."

"Thank you, Chef Soltner," says the young man. Before letting him leave, André advises him not to quit his current job until he has a new one. "This is a tough time for restaurants," André says.

Looking grim, the young man says, "I know," and leaves.

"It's unbelievable how many people are looking for work," André says as he turns and walks up the stairs to his third-floor office.

Simple and functional, it looks more like a grammar school principal's office than that of a high-profile chef. But giving away its owner's occupation are a large yellow stuffed duck wearing a white apron, a chef's hat and a white name tag saying "Chef Béarnaise," a shelf full of cookbooks, and a few framed cooking awards. The duck was given to André years ago by the young daughter of steady patrons. Two clean, empty wineglasses stand on the desk, awaiting the glass supplier who will be arriving later.

Since only André's staff and his suppliers ever see his office, he sees no need to spend money on sprucing the place up. André sits behind his plain desk, with his back to two small windows, and I sit in one of the two hard-backed wooden chairs facing his desk. André picks up the phone and calls the chef at Prunelle to ask if he would participate in a promotion for Alsace. The chef agrees. Then he calls another chef to talk about where to hold the annual meeting of the Maîtres Cuisiniers de France, the prestigious French chef/owners association of which André has been president since 1973.

His third call is to a man who repairs his ovens but has no idea how to repair the combi oven in the prep kitchen. André tells the repairman that he has made arrangements for him to go up to Vermont for two days to observe how the ovens are built.

The fourth call is to one of his largest wine suppliers, Wine Markets International. The supplier must have said, "How's life?" because André now replies, "Life is good." He listens for a moment and then says, "It will be even shittier when you hear what I have to tell you. When Bob came in to sell us wine I didn't buy. You were always reasonable in your prices but you are not anymore. I bought a case of 1963 port from you and paid one thousand fifty dollars for it. One week ago I wanted two more cases and saw you are asking four hundred dollars more per case."

André listens and then says, "Yeah. But the customer doesn't want to know how and why. They only care about how much they pay and I'm calling to tell you that you are charging four hundred dollars more."

Again André listens and says, "Yeah, but I never bought by the bottle. . . . No, I am not interested at these prices." He listens some more and scans other prices on the list. "I look now at the Cabernet, which, with the discount, you ask a hundred and forty dollars. I pay one hundred twenty dollars at Château and Estate. . . . I am not complaining because I didn't buy it from you. You didn't get me with these prices."

André's phone beeps and he asks the supplier to "hold one second."

He takes the other phone call, from his linen company, and asks that person to "hold one second" too. He goes back to the wine distributor and says, "I just wanted you to be aware. I didn't buy and I wanted to tell you the reason. Now I have to go. I have another phone call."

He picks up the other line and says, "Ed, I left messages for you yesterday. Didn't you get them? . . . Look, Ed. Your company makes me sick. On Saturday no one picks up the linen. Tuesday the guy comes in and he hollers because the other guy didn't take it. He would take only two packages. The rest stayed here and were picked up today."

He listens and then says, "There is no one to talk to. You have to take your son to the hospital, so it's understandable why you are not there. I ask for [someone else] and he's on Long Island. It not only bothers me that the linen has been sitting here but your linen gets spoiled when this happens."

Again he listens and replies, "No. I don't have a problem with the guy who came on Tuesday. I have a problem with the guy who didn't come on Saturday. Your man from Tuesday said he had a problem all over. He had to pick up the Saturday linen every-where.

"My next problem. You take jackets away. The special jackets. And these don't come back. Yesterday only three or four came back from seven or eight. Yesterday I took two jackets from my own stock. I still had them from France. But something is wrong there, Jesus, Mother, Joseph."

It is common knowledge in the restaurant industry that a restaurant has little, if any, say in who its linen (and dairy) supplier—or its garbage collector—will be. Although André claims he could switch his linen supplier and his other service companies at any time, other restaurateurs, such as Gisele Masson at La Grenouille, have said that when it comes to these areas of the restaurant industry, their hands are tied. "You're married to your linen company," Gisele Masson says. "You can't think of changing, and if you *do,* the first linen company will say to the second, 'Give me back my territory.' The same is true for dairy and garbage. Just try changing your garbage collector."

André says he's never felt the need to change his dairy and garbage companies and also claims never to have been affected by the bribery and corruption some restaurateurs say are endemic in the industry. At La Grenouille, Charles Masson, Jr., claims that some members of all restaurant-associated professions, ranging from food critics to suppliers to the guys who give out parking tickets in front of a restaurant, are involved in a large system of bribery and kickbacks.

André, however, says, "I can assure you that I heard a lot of stories but never anybody directly or indirectly asked me [for] anything. I heard stories like you but I had never, never any problems. People say, 'Have you ever had problems with the Mafia or anything?' In thirty years I have never had any problems. If you are not looking for it, it doesn't come to you."

Although André claims never to have been solicited for a bribe, a 1988 article in *Long Island Newsday*'s Sunday magazine claims otherwise. The writer overheard "someone . . . putting the arm on André Soltner."

In the article, the reporter witnessed André take a phone call and then look "concerned, then irritated. 'No way,' he says. *'Nothing over the phone.* Nothing over the phone. Talk to my lawyer. Why? Because it's the way we do things.' He hangs up. 'That was the "police," he says. He makes a face. 'Some phony guy. He wants $150 for some kind of inspection approval.' "

One of the worst stories about corrupt restaurant inspectors was told by Barry and Susan Wine, owners of the famed Quilted Giraffe (which closed in December 1992), in a 1988 letter to *The New York Times*. *Nation's Restaurant News,* a trade journal, ran an article about this letter, reporting the following:

At the Quilted Giraffe, the dining-room staff shared its tips with the kitchen workers. The New York State Department of Labor once investigated the policy to make sure everything was on the up-and-up. It was. But during the probe the Wines were approached by a Labor Department investigator who "thought he might be of help in settling our case," Wine wrote in her letter to *The New York Times*.

The investigator, according to Wine, "had a little business on the side, selling coffee to restaurants. He offered to sell us coffee at $15 a pound. He suggested the first order be for 100 pounds."

"Through their lawyer, the Wines reported the attempted shake-down to the inspector's supervisor," *NRN* reported. "Instead of being thanked for alerting the department to possible corruption, the Wines were subjected to harassment.

"The hearing officer in the tip-sharing investigation 'closed ranks with his buddies, refused to listen to our case, and indicated he would find against us,' Wine recalled in her letter. 'Soon the same agency invented a second violation and gladly made all files relating to the supposed violations—which they now termed "misappropriation" to make it appear my husband was stealing money from our own waiters—available to the press, where the accusations of impropriety were retold in full color with photos.'

"Even after Wine reported the matter to the Federal Bureau of Investigation, the inspector with the coffee business was allowed to remain on the job," according to *NRN*. He wasn't dismissed or prosecuted, just temporarily suspended.

" 'Not only did I not get a thank you; I got a kick in the abdomen,' Wine wrote. 'I now have what seems to be [a] never-ending battle with this department. They are mad at me for turning in one of their guys. . . .

" 'Too often,' Wine continued, 'if bribe solicitation is taking place at the investigator or inspector level, supervisory personnel, reaching into high levels in such departments, are involved. In such cases attempting to report the solicitation can be fraught with real risk of retaliation as the department seeks to cover up.' "

Hoping to get André to reveal some of his own brushes with corruption, I show him this article. He reads it but still insists, "I'm thirty years here and I've never had the slightest problem. I've never had anyone coming in looking for money, never any problems. I heard about [what happened at the Quilted Giraffe] and things like that but I've never had them happen to me."

The intercom on André's phone buzzes and he's told he has two visitors waiting for him. On the way down, he says that the aggravation of getting after people to do their jobs right—like the linen guy—never stops. "Nothing is ever done right the first time," he says. "What does it say about people and how they see their jobs?"

As for the liquor distributor, he says, "If you don't check their prices all the time and just keep on ordering from them, they will take advantage of you."

Downstairs, a young American woman and a Japanese man who is producing a video for Japan on top American restaurants are waiting in the bar. The woman asks André if she can give the Japanese man a tour. "Sure," says André. He follows them, listening, as they walk through his restaurant.

"Here's the bar," the young woman says. "And here's the open kitchen so that they can be in touch with the customers. And here [in the first dining room], look at this mirror. It looks like a frame but it is painted on the wall." Walking into the garden room, she says, "And this dining room gives you the feeling of being in an outdoor garden which, in New York, especially in the winter, is a real treat."

"It used to be an outdoor garden but we enclosed it because of the weather," says André.

They go up to the second floor, where the woman asks André

which dining room is for smokers and which for nonsmokers. André gets them mixed up and then corrects himself—the rear room is for smokers. (On both floors the smaller dining room is for smoking.)

The woman asks the Japanese man if he has any questions, and he asks, "What is the thought behind the food?"

It takes a while for the woman and André to understand what he is saying. "Thought," says the Japanese man, pointing to his forehead.

"I think he means what is the philosophy behind the food," says the woman.

"No philosophy," says André. His visitors look disappointed. André seems curt in not expounding a bit on his approach to cooking, but he's telling it the way he sees it. He is not an introspective or philosophical man, and he doesn't think much about the kind of food he serves. He just cooks what he likes.

"Any trick to it being so good?" says the woman.

"No tricks," says André. "Just being here all the time." With that one sentence he reveals what he genuinely believes to be the one and only secret to his success, but his visitors look insulted and say they have no more questions. After they leave André heads back up to his office to meet William Kelly, the vice president of sales at Minners Designs, from whom André orders his Christofle silverware, Woodmere china, and Minners glassware.

André picks up the two glasses standing on his desk and, holding out first one glass and then the other, says to Kelly, "I ordered one size glass and have been delivered a carton of this size. You are good with selling and good at sending the bill. But in between I get nothing."

Kelly takes André's anger in stride. He simply apologizes for the mixup and says a carton of glasses of the right size will be sent.

Later Kelly says to me, "It's like Murphy's Law, this business. If it can go wrong, it will. André's got his hands in a lot of things. He's a very professional person but he must be under a lot of pressure with all the nonsense that goes on in the press about being number one and not being number one. The last thing he needs is to get wrong-size glasses. It's an annoyance to him."

Kelly leaves and André spends the rest of the hour before five P.M. planning the menus for three upcoming parties. Two of the menus are for the French ambassador to the United Nations. The third is for "a stock-market guy."

André writes a tentative menu on a legal pad, saying, "I can't be sure that the ambassador will agree to this menu, but I have to be ready to know what to tell him. It doesn't mean he'll take my suggestion. I may suggest pumpkin soup and he might say, 'No. It's cream. I don't want cream.'"

André calls the ambassador but his secretary says he doesn't have time to talk to him right now. "It's always like that with ambassadors," says André. "They want to plan a party and then they never have time to do it."

André's menu planning is punctuated with calls—one from *The New York Times* asking who sells him frogs' legs and several from suppliers. As these latter phone calls come in, André begins to have a sense of which foods will and will not be available for him tomorrow. He will plan or change tomorrow's specials accordingly.

If this was a Friday afternoon, André would also be planning the lunch specials for next week. He does this the same way every Friday, starting by writing "Tuesday, Wednesday, Thursday, Friday" down the left side of a legal pad. Since lunch is not served on Mondays or Saturdays, these days do not appear on his list.

André then opens a black-and-white composition book, the same kind that is used to log orders downstairs. For years, at the end of every week, he's recorded in this notebook appetizer and entrée specials he's prepared and liked. To draw inspiration for the coming week he leafs through the notebook.

The names of the dishes, with no descriptions, are listed in his rounded European handwriting, one after another, for pages. These names get André thinking about what he'd like to eat next week. His wanting to eat these dishes himself is the primary influence on what he will offer in the restaurant.

"The most important thing for me when I plan the plats du jour," says André, "is that I want to eat them myself. Maybe I haven't had something for a long time and am in the mood for it.

"Other times I try making a dish that I had in a restaurant [over summer vacation] and liked. Or else I look for new recipes. I read cookbooks and get ideas. We do things in our interpretation but we don't create from scratch. What else can you do with potatoes? Everything possible has been tried. I don't like to say we can create something. I look in books and that gives me ideas about what we knew before but maybe haven't thought about." André owns about two hundred cookbooks, ranging from rare cookbooks written by Carême to more recent ones by chefs Joel Robuchon and Jean-Georges Vongerichten.

While André won't admit to being directly influenced by the food he ate at Vongerichten's New York City restaurant, Jo-Jo, last July, Vongerichten's cookbook *Simple Cuisine* sits on André's desk. When pressed about it, André says, "I cook for forty-two years and you look a little bit at what the others do but you don't change as easy."

Sometimes, too, what will be cooked is influenced by customers who, when they make their reservations, say they'd like André to make them a particular dish. Their request might appeal to André so much that he will make the dish available for everyone in the restaurant.

No matter what the source of his inspiration, André always plans the appetizer and the main course to complement each other. Tuesdays through Thursdays the main course special is always meat, and therefore the appetizer is always fish. Every Friday the main course is fish, so the appetizer is meat. Offering fish on Fridays "comes from my childhood, when my mother always served fish on Friday," says André. "Back then Friday was the day the fish stores were best supplied because the Catholics would all eat fish on Fridays. I am Protestant but still my mother knew the fish would be fresh on Fridays and so she always made it. And I continue to do the same."

While André was working in his office, his secretaries down the hall were taking the calls for reservations. All of the captains and most of the waiters are out on their two-hour break.

The two waiters who are here are setting up the dining rooms in the same manner as they were set up this morning. Pierre spent the hour between three and four restocking the bar and compiling his list of which wines were sold. He'll refer to this list tomorrow morning when he does inventory. Jacques, meanwhile, assembled a roast pork dish for tomorrow's staff lunch so that tomorrow morning all he'll have to do is put it in the oven. He then diced onions, leeks, and celery and cleaned split peas for tomorrow's soups. Later, he checked the inventory of dairy products and vegetables and ordered these for tomorrow.

By four in the afternoon, Henry, the fish cook, has joined George, Denis, and Stuart in the upstairs kitchen, and Jacques, Mirielle, Pierre, Bill, and Joe, as well as the other prep-kitchen workers, have gone home, leaving the prep kitchen shiny clean and ready for tomorrow. The only sign that any of them were ever there is a new version of Bill's "to do" list, posted above his workstation.

George's last task before dinner service begins is making hollandaise sauce. Half of this will be served as pure hollandaise. The other half will be mixed with a reduction of tomato and tarragon purees to make *sauce choron.*

As he separates eggs, George tells me, "The whites are for Stuart to use for the soufflé." Then, as everyone else has done at one point or another, he points out the frugality of the restaurant, saying, "We use everything. Nothing goes to waste. The whites are for Stuart and the eggshells are for Billy for his garden."

He places the egg yolks and a drop each of water and vinegar in a large metal bowl, which he then puts on the hot corner of the stove, rather than directly over the flame. "We don't want to make an omelette so we don't want it to be too hot," he says as he starts whisking the sauce.

He whisks nonstop for the next ten to fifteen minutes. When the yolks start getting too warm he removes the bowl from the heat and places it on the counter until the temperature falls. Then he puts the bowl back on the stove. Perpetually whisking, he continues moving back and forth from the stove to the counter until the yolks' volume has increased and their consistency has thickened to the point where they stay on the whisk and the bottom of the bowl becomes visible. When this happens he adds warm clarified butter and explains that the temperature must be watched very carefully or else the sauce won't work. I ask if this is the hardest thing to cook, and he says no, the hardest thing is "cooking just right—not to overcook or undercook. Cooking steak perfectly rare is hard."

$\mathscr{S}$OUFFLÉ GLACÉ AUX FRAMBOISES

FROZEN RASPBERRY SOUFFLÉ

FOR 12 PEOPLE

For the *fonds de succes* (almond meringue):

5 egg whites
1 cup sugar

1¾ cups sliced almonds
(puree in food
processor until very
fine)

For the raspberry layer:

1 lb. white sugar
½ pint water
10 egg whites

1 pint fresh or frozen
raspberries, pureed
(if using frozen
raspberries, thaw first
and drain all liquid)
Juice of 2 lemons
1 pint heavy cream

Line a 2-quart soufflé mold with an unbuttered 4-inch-wide strip of waxed paper. Secure the ends with tape. The paper should extend about 3 inches above the mold.

Preheat oven to 200 degrees. Beat 5 egg whites until they are stiff. Mix in 1 cup of sugar and the almonds. Line a cookie sheet with waxed paper. Spread the mixture on the waxed paper in a ¼-inch layer. Bake for about 1½ hours until golden brown.

Cook 1 pound of sugar in ½ pint water until temperature on a candy thermometer reaches 260 degrees and the sugar has become a syrup. Whisk 10 egg whites stiff, and slowly pour the cooked syrup over them while continuing to whisk until the syrup is cold. Gradually whisk in the raspberry puree and the juice of two lemons. Fold in one pint of heavy cream. Avoid overmixing.

Using a spoon, spread one third of the raspberry mixture on the bottom of the soufflé dish. Cover this with one half of the almond meringue. Add another raspberry layer, then the rest of the meringue, and then the remaining raspberry mixture. You will have three raspberry layers and two meringue layers.

Freeze for at least three hours. Remove waxed paper from soufflé dish before serving. Soufflé can be made two days in advance and stored in the freezer until needed.

NOTE: A long-running favorite at the restaurant.

5:00 P.M.

As he does every day at this time, André leaves his office and goes to the second-story dining room to have dinner with Simone. "We talk about phone calls, orders, cleaning supplies, the fact that we work too much," he says. They sit down at a table and are served by a waiter.

The dining-room staff have returned from their break and, along with the kitchen staff, are eating in the downstairs front dining room. Sitting and eating in this civilized manner helps the kitchen staff recharge, preparing them for the grueling work ahead. Cooking dinner is at least twice as much work as lunch since there are two dinner seatings and customers often order more courses.

After they are finished, the dining-room staff, all of whom had donned street clothes for their two-hour break, change back into their work uniforms and the kitchen staff return to the stoves. George carries in a silver bucket filled with ice cubes and puts it on a shelf above the counter across from Denis's stove. Because of the heat from the stoves, the ice will quickly melt into cold water. Over the course of the evening, the kitchen workers will constantly ladle refreshing glasses of ice-cold water from this bucket. Each worker has claimed a glass for himself, which he will use over and over again.

A few minutes later, the dining-room staff once again stand at the ready to receive customers. The captains are at the same stations they worked at lunch; the waiters have rotated.

Luc remains at the back tables in the downstairs dining room. René and Jean Louis are now working the front tables downstairs, and the waiters who had that station at lunch are upstairs. Those who had been upstairs are now working with Luc.

The night bartender is behind the bar and Simone is at the hostess station, where she receives a phone call from a regular customer asking if he can expand his eight o'clock reservation from eight to ten people. "Of course," Simone says, never letting on that this request will cause a significant problem.

A round table that will seat no more than eight people had been set up in the downstairs front room for this man's party. To accommodate his request, two tables for four and one for two now have to be moved out of the rear dining room and pushed together to seat ten in the front room. Since André doesn't want his staff moving tables around when customers are already in the restaurant, this will take three tables out of circulation for both seatings. This is not a problem for the six o'clock seating, since it is not full. It could, however, become a big problem for the eight o'clock one, which *is* completely booked, especially if everyone from the second seating arrives on time and if members of the first seating linger over dessert. This is the one and only time André actually hopes that some people won't show up for their reservations. If that happens, then seating will go off without a hitch.

André tells the captains what tonight's specials are, and then he asks the dining-room staff, and the cooks, to be on their toes because of the possible table shortage. "We all have to move a little faster," he says. They nod and return to their posts.

DINNER

At the stoves "the line" (restaurant terminology for the staff members who cook the meals) has formed and is ready to begin its adrenaline-driven task of getting the food out.

The line in restaurant kitchens usually consists of three people lined up in order of seniority. As they face the stoves, the person on the right (George) has the highest rank and cooks the meat. The one in the middle (Henry) cooks the fish. The one on the left (Denis) pours the soups and also cooks the hot appetizers, vegetables, and noodles.

Separated from Denis by the small face-level oven used for baking appetizers and soufflés and warming the breads is Stuart. On his left, facing a sink that runs the length of the narrow wall at the left end of the kitchen, is the potwasher. Behind Stuart stands another kitchen worker, who will be manning the two small dishwashing machines, one on top of the counter, the other underneath. To deal with the minor flooding the washing will produce, both these men are standing on top of large flattened cardboard cartons. Three small drains are cut into the red clay tile floor to catch any severe overflow.

André stands framed by the kitchen window so that he will be in plain sight of the customers. His hands must always be busy, and right now they are hard at work making tiny carrot shavings with a small sharp knife. These shavings will be used to garnish tomorrow's chicken soup.

If André has nothing to do, his fingers start tapping impatiently, as if spelling out in Morse code "Give me something to do, give me something to chop, give me someone's hand to shake." Unlike André, the other cooks stand still, momentarily unoccupied as they wait for the doors to open. All of them are wearing white long-sleeved cotton jackets, black-and-white checked pants, knee-length aprons tied on at the waist, kerchiefs around their necks, and, except for George (who wears white sneakers), black rubber-soled shoes. The dishwashers are bare-headed; André and the cooks all wear toques.

The food is all in its proper place, in the refrigerators, in freezers, in canisters by the stove or on the counters. The soups and sauces have all been poured into metal canisters positioned between George's and Henry's stoves, and each canister has its own ladle. Underneath the long window, through which the hot appetizers and all the entrées will be passed to the waiters, are rows of little bowls filled with garnishes, such as chopped almonds, shallots, parsley, tomato, and watercress.

The counters are clean, the floor is spotless, and their jackets are sparkling white. Not for long . . .

5:45 P.M.

*T*he door is unlocked and tonight's first customers arrive. The nighttime coat check woman takes their coats and Simone, in her singsong voice, says, *"Bon soir, monsieur, bon soir, madame."*

As the kitchen waits for the first food orders to arrive, Henry talks about a recent dinner he had at Le Comptoir, a new and already trendy restaurant. "The place was filled with models," he says. "It was jammed."

Henry, who started working here in 1984 and before that was at La Côte Basque for five years, loves to gossip. He is always ready to talk about a new restaurant, a restaurant review, a feature article on a restaurant, or a fellow member of the restaurant world. Next to André, I found Henry the most hospitable person here, always offering me food or drink and, if I refused, pressing me to tell him what I had for lunch or dinner.

He is very much a part of the young New York social scene, hanging out in hip restaurants and, in the summer, the hippest beach in the Hamptons. His love of the scene makes him seem younger than he is—even he seems surprised by his age. "I'm thirty-five," he says, "and I feel like a teenager. When I think about it, I think, Where did those years go? I know where they went. I spent them in the kitchen.

"The restaurant business is brutal. You work such long hours. Ten years went by so fast. You work hard, but by Saturday night you're ready, because you know you have your day off. In the summer we have weekends off so you know what it feels like to have . . ."

"A life?" I fill in for him when he pauses.

He laughs. "You sound like my girlfriend," he says. " 'Don't you want a life?' " he says, imitating a woman's voice.

Right now, however, his life obviously revolves around the restaurant world. Henry tells André about another restaurant that was negatively reviewed in *New York Newsday*. André asks Henry to show him the review later and Henry nods. Looking at my notepad and then at me, André says, "Don't become a critic."

Even though food writers and restaurant reviewers have showered André and his restaurant with almost nothing but praise, he does not reciprocate in kind.

"The food writers are out to get us," he says. (By "us" he means restaurateurs in general.) "Many times they are not fair with us. They work for their image, for themselves. One day, and I was not involved, thank God, but a writer, he went around to the restaurants and asked to use the bathroom. But he was not a customer. Some said, 'Go to hell.' Others let him use the bathroom, and he put a big story in a magazine about it. It was in the article which restaurant said, 'Go to hell.'

"That's not fair. I was not involved but I could have been involved. I could have come out beautiful. Maybe if we were not busy I would have said, 'Be my guest. Please.' But maybe if I had a lot of customers around me and was busy, under pressure, I would have said, 'Can you not go [leave the restaurant]?' And I am still the same guy, you know?"

Like most restaurateurs, André has not kept his feelings about restaurant reviewers a secret. He once told *Newsday:* "Sometimes I resent that after forty years in this business I have to wait for marks like a schoolboy, from people than whom I know ten times more about cooking."

Who are the critics, these people who hold what seem to be the most wonderful jobs in the world? What are their qualifications? What factors do they weigh when deciding whether to give a good or bad review? Here's a look at how one of the more powerful reviewers in New York City works and what she has to say about Lutèce:

Gael Greene has been restaurant reviewer for *New York* magazine since 1970. She grew up in Detroit and majored in English at the University of Michigan. As a sophomore she went to Paris and "discovered great food." After graduating she moved to New York and got a job on the general assignment desk of the *New York Post,* where, as she says, she "covered plane crashes, murders, queens who visited, mothers of killers, dead people." She then became a free-lancer, writing "anything anyone asked me to." She educated herself about food, taking courses, reading, cooking, and going to restaurants.

As a free-lancer she interviewed Craig Claiborne for *Look* magazine, and when she herself became a critic, she followed his rules, which, she says, "he basically made up himself.

"When I interviewed him, he told me how he did it. He went a minimum of three times and took friends with him. The *Times* paid for everything. He was the first restaurant critic who treated everything quite seriously, did not accept free meals, paid his own way, and was anonymous if possible. He always waited three or four weeks, until a restaurant had shaken down somewhat, before he went to review. That's my practice also."

Before she even enters a restaurant she's reviewing, she says, "I notice what's happening on the street. If there's a lineup of limos and fancy antique cars and so on, I can't help but notice that. If there's garbage by the entrance or bums on the steps, I would notice that too. I might look in to see how it looks from the outside.

"Inside, the first thing I notice is the smell: Is there a strong butter smell or delicious garlic cooking in butter or oil? Or is the smell unpleasant, like stale or rancid oil or over-the-hill fish? I'm aware of whether or not someone is there to greet you. How long do you have to wait? Is it crowded at the door? Is there room to stand and wait? Where is the coat check? How long is the coat check taking? Who's in the restaurant? What's the crowd like? What's the lighting like? If there are great flowers, that's an exciting beginning.

"When I'm seated I'm interested in how the table looks and feels and the condition of the menu. Is it too big? Hard to read? Dirty? Misspelled? Is the language too pretentious or is it not translated, which I think is outrageous at this time in New York. I would think we would all be over that snobbery. If the tabletop accessories are special, of course I see that right away. If they're ordinary, they don't register immediately. If the tablecloth is linen or hand-laundered I'll see that immediately. The rest might come later.

"I see how long the wait is for a drink, water, service. Whether there's any kind of offering on the table or something that comes while you're waiting. Is the service professional? How do I feel in the place? Do I feel good here? Is the service welcoming and warm, or indifferent and arrogant?

"How does the food look on the plate when it's delivered? Is the plate so hot I can burn myself if I accidentally touch it? Is water replenished? Do they offer more bread if the bread disappears? Does anyone remember which customer gets what? A lot of restaurants have a two-platoon system—one waiter takes the order and another delivers it. I'm interested to see if they can get four dishes on the table in the same minute. I see if the waiter asks who gets what and then puts it down in the wrong place anyway. The pacing of the meal is important. So is whether things are cooked the way we requested them. I think a glorious dessert can leave you with a nice feeling even if the rest of the meal was ordinary. Of course, all would be forgiven if the food was wonderful and price was right."

Greene usually brings four or more people with her when she's reviewing, so she usually tastes almost everything on a typical menu. She eats out seven nights and two or three lunch hours a week. "I try to go once or twice a year to places that I love," she says. "I feel so jealous of my readers, who get to just go to places they want to go to. Three to four nights in a row I have disappointing meals."

How does she feel about Lutèce? "Lutèce is not fun or lively or the place to see faces in *Women's Wear Daily*," she says. "The excitement there has always been the food and special things that André Soltner might do for a regular. I have friends who used to go there every other Monday and just say, 'Cook for us.' He would dream up wonderful things for them."

This comment once again illustrates the efficacy of André's "Today I can make for you . . ." approach. Never would he make special dishes for only one table on such a regular basis. Whatever André "dreamed up," he dreamed up for all of his customers. Yet Greene's friends were made to feel it was being done just for them. It is truly astonishing how nourished and special a touch of hospitality, and the right few words, can make people feel.

Even Molly O'Neill, when she was a restaurant reviewer at *New York Newsday,* wrote that André's "custom cooking is the thread that wove the legend of Lutèce." She described the dishes André made for "well-known guests" and complained that "André doesn't cook for me." If André offered a dish to "well-known guests," he would offer it to everyone as part of the daily specials that don't appear on the menu.

O'Neill obviously doesn't love the dishes Lutèce offers on its menu. Nor does Jane Freiman of *Newsday* or Greene. "The things he's kept on the menu are so old hat and boring," she told me. "Like the beef Wellington. The last time I was there beef Wellington was still on the menu. For a long time his mind was closed to the revolution in cooking. We would tell him about the excitement of just-cooked fish or barely cooked chicken. He would put it down." Good thing, too, in view of what we know now about bacterial contamination in fish and salmonella in chicken.

"He was trained in the old style," Greene says. "It's hard for him to be persuaded to move away from tradition. He's moved away a little, but he still does a lot of the old traditional things."

Greene's comment illustrates an attitude food writer Mimi Sheraton once described: "Last year's Beef Wellington has about as much appeal to a food journalist as last year's A-line dress has to a fashion editor, and so chefs, like couturiers, now have to come up with a new line every year."

André's response? "No matter what they say about wanting light food and liking new dishes, guests love the old tastes." And staunchly, steadfastly, he refuses to get rid of them, being more concerned about pleasing his customers than the critics.

Although the general public wouldn't recognize a food critic even if he or she was seated at the same table, restaurateurs often do. Greene says she retains her anonymity only about 25 percent of the time, and when the restaurateur doesn't know her, other patrons "love to be the one to tell the owner who you are."

André says he knows "the ones who have been around for a long time—Mimi Sheraton, Bryan Miller, or Gael Greene." But when I ask how well he "knows" them, he says not very well at all.

"It's a little like a barrier with the food writers. We don't socialize with any food writers and we never did. We have certain ones who we like because they write nice things about us but we have no very friendly rapport with them because they are in a situation and we are in a situation where even if we respect each other we cannot socialize. I have friends that I can invite over for Sunday dinner. Even if I would like to invite a food writer, I don't want to try because I don't know his reaction. He can say to me, 'You're trying to bribe me.' There might be a feeling that I do it to influence them. They can't accept it either because it's a conflict of interest. It's difficult for us and for them. We respect each other and we stay at a distance."

As for the lesser-known critics, and even sometimes the gurus, he says, "My wife many times doesn't recognize them. She's busy and she doesn't care. Sometimes they are recognized by the staff and sometimes not at all."

Someone recently said to me that even if a restaurateur didn't know a critic by sight, the manner in which those at the table ordered and/or ate would be a dead giveaway, since it's not often that one person at one table tastes *all* the dishes. Wouldn't this recognition, this person wondered, of necessity make the owner and/or chef pay more attention to this table's food and service?

To be sure, the service in most restaurants could definitely be made better if the service staff was alerted to the presence of a reviewer. "We can give a little more attention by service," says André. "Of course I wouldn't say to my staff, 'The heck with this one.' I would say, 'Be careful.' But that's about all that we can do. Many times when someone like that is in here, my staff is nervous and they drop a plate, bang. So, many times I don't tell my staff when I've recognized a critic."

Although service could be improved, the taste and quality of the food couldn't be changed since, as we've seen from this day at Lutèce, many of the dishes have been assembled in advance. Even if André wanted to change something, he wouldn't be able to.

★ ★ ★ ★

Back in Lutèce's kitchen the first dinner order has been stuck onto the spike inside the long window across from the stoves.

Henry removes the slip and calls out the entire order in a monotone. Although they will start working on the appetizers now, Henry calls out the entrées too, in case any of these dishes need a long time to cook.

On the white order form, the captain has written the table number in the upper left-hand corner and the numeral "four" in the upper right, signifying that this order is for four people.

The order is written as follows, with the number on the left signifying the quantity ordered. The number on the right is the seat number. Seat numbers are given only for the appetizers; the rest of the courses are listed in the same order of seating:

1 artichaut [artichoke]	1
1 gambas [jumbo shrimp with saffron sauce]	2
1 pâté	4
1 huître [oysters]	3

Then, with a space between courses, comes:

1 fillet of veal
1 canard 2 ["2" signifies that the duck serves two people]
1 venison stew

Another line is skipped between these offerings and the next listing:

2 asparagus vinaigrette
2 salade mix

Unless the table requests otherwise, the salads and asparagus are served as side dishes to the main course.

After he's finished reading the entire order, Henry slides the slip into an overhead slot in front of the long window. Everyone in the kitchen knows that any orders still on the spike have not yet been started, whereas any orders in this slot are in various stages of preparation. Once the appetizers have been given to the waiters, they will be crossed off the order slip and the order will be placed back in the overhead slot. As soon as the kitchen begins working on the entrées, the order goes onto a white board lying on the right side of the window ledge. This board has fifteen vertical spikes sticking up from it. After the entrées have gone out, the order slips move on to a second single spike, this one on the right side of the long window.

Now that an order has arrived, the cooks immediately get to work. Knowing that the duck takes about forty minutes to cook, George puts it in the oven as Stuart and Henry begin assembling or cooking the appetizers. The gambas fall under Henry's jurisdiction because they are seafood.

As Stuart puts an artichoke on a plate, Henry puts the gambas in the oven and ladles some of the saffron sauce he made this afternoon into a skillet and heats the sauce. He then turns to the oysters, which Guido opened this morning. Although earlier Henry chopped leeks, which will be used as a bed for the oysters, the sauce—made from oyster juice, white wine, and heavy cream—could not be made in advance.

Stuart in the meantime has pulled the pâté *en croûte* out of the refrigerator and cut a slice of it. He puts his two filled plates on the ledge in the window in the door. When Henry's dishes are ready, he puts them on the ledge in the long window. The waiter whisks the four plates away.

As the orders come in, Henry or George—whoever is free—reads them out loud and slips them into the overhead slot. The pace begins to pick up.

The chefs work mainly on soups and appetizers until the waiter who brought the first order returns to the window and calls out, "You can go with table nine." This means that table is ready to eat its entrées.

Since the entrées for the first order are all meat or poultry, they fall under George's jurisdiction. The only other person involved in assembling the plates for this table is Denis, who sautés all the vegetables and noodles. He knows that the venison stew and the duck are always served with spaetzle and the fillet of veal with mixed vegetables. The spaetzle and vegetables have been cooked in advance, and now Denis needs to sauté them in butter. Before beginning, however, he waits for the go-ahead from George, who is checking the duck. Since meat has the longest cooking time, both Denis and Henry always take their cooking cues from George to ensure that all of their dishes will be ready at the same time.

The duck is almost ready and so George nods at Denis, who starts sautéing. George, in the meantime, puts the veal in the oven and dishes out the venison stew into a small pot and places that on top of the stove to heat up.

He takes the duck out of the oven, places it on a silver serving platter, and passes it through the window to the waiter, who takes it out to present it to customers. While the duck is being presented, George slices the veal and arranges the slices on the plate next to the portion of spaetzle Denis has served. He then places the plate on top of one of the two open broilers hanging on the wall behind the stoves so that the rising heat from the broilers will keep the food warm.

The waiter brings the duck back to the kitchen and André carves it. At one time the carving was done in the dining room, but it's done in the kitchen now to expedite and better control the timing of service. "We can tell if the person wants a big show," says André. "If they do, then the waiter carves it at the table." Otherwise the carved duck goes out with the rest of the finished dishes.

When André is finished with the duck, George dishes out the venison stew, and all the dishes are put out on the ledge for the waiter to take.

Denis and George both bring the pans they used for cooking to the potwasher, who is completely focused on the sink, washing quickly, efficiently, his bare hands turning pink and puckered in the hot water. Pots are never reused without being washed first, even if they are being used for the same food.

The dishwasher is scraping the dirty plates the busboys continually pass through the small hip-high window to the left of the dishwashing machine and stacking the dishes and glasses in the machine. While it runs through its short cycle, he dries pots for the potwasher. When the cycle is finished, the dishwasher quickly opens the cover, ignoring the steam that hits him in the face. He swiftly unloads the clean plates, replaces them with dirty ones, and starts the next cycle.

Noticing me watching these workers, André says, "They are very important guys in this organization. Of course, every restaurant pays its chefs well. Good ones are scarce. But to appreciate the difference at Lutèce, you must look at how we treat the dishwasher. It's worth it to pay that person fifty or a hundred dollars more a week than another restaurant might. A careless dishwasher can break twenty dishes in an evening. But, if treated well, he will be more careful. And he will make the effort to get the dishes out faster. Then the chef can send the meals out faster, the waiters can bring the food faster, and the customer is more satisfied—all because of the dishwasher."

As the number of orders picks up, so do the concentration and noise levels. The sounds are numerous but they somehow blend into one: running water, scouring powder on metal, banging of pots against the inside of the sink as they're rinsed, clanging as the cooks stack dirty pans on the counters behind them, clanking of plates as they come out of the dishwasher, Stuart's knife chopping, the hiss of oil as it misses a pan and hits the flames.

As the cooking of appetizers for some tables starts to overlap with the cooking of entrées for others, André begins to cook some of the entrées, working at George's stove. This is the least utilized stove since most of the meats are roasted in the oven.

As the pace increases, the cooks no longer bring their pans to the potwasher after each entrée is done. Instead, they put them on the counter across from the stoves, and when his two machines are progressing through their cycles, the dishwasher makes a run through the kitchen every ten minutes or so to help out his co-worker and pick up the dirty pans.

Of all the cooks, George seems to have the most physically demanding job. He is constantly running up and down the steps to use the combi oven in the prep kitchen, where the baby lamb, the chickens, and the squabs are cooked. All of these do better if they are "baked with some humidity," says André.

Like the ducks, the orders for rack of lamb, pheasant, and whole baby chickens are put in the oven as soon as orders for them arrive, and George sets a timer for five minutes earlier than the scheduled completion time for each. "It's better to wait for it to finish cooking than to overcook it," he says.

There is one good thing about having to run downstairs all the time, however. It gives George a respite from the heat of the kitchen. Earlier, André had called me over to stand by one of the stoves for a second. "I want you to feel how hot it is here," he said. It was *very* hot.

As the last of the dinner orders for the first seating filter in, Stuart is busily slicing and scooping desserts. These orders are left on the spike on the ledge of the window cut into the kitchen door. This door is directly across from Stuart's station.

Stuart removes the slips immediately, and as soon as he starts working on the orders, he puts the slips under the spike. He puts the soufflé orders, which the waiters take at the beginning of the meal, on the spike on the shelf above his station. Stuart pours the soufflé batter into the molds immediately but he doesn't put them in the oven until the waiter, knowing that the table has been served its entrées, tells him to do so.

André, who seems to have eyes in back of his head and knows what everyone is doing or has forgotten to do and which table's order they are working on, sees Stuart take two soufflés out of the oven. André takes some raspberry sauce and writes "Steve" on one soufflé and "Lutèce" on the other.

As he does this, he says, "The wife will say, 'Why didn't you write my name on mine?' and I'll say, 'I didn't want to play a joke like that on you.' But really I don't remember the wife's name."

To the left of the dishwasher, the dirty plates are piled high. Henry, who is between orders, walks over to the stack and picks up some of the plates, checking to see if the food has been completely eaten. "That's the only way you can tell if they liked it," he says.

Pointing to a plate with a half-eaten gambas shell on it, he says, "This person liked it. They even ate the shell."

Looking at the plates may be the only way Henry can tell if people liked what he prepared, but André gets more direct and immediate reinforcement since he's able to stroll through the dining room whenever he wants to—or is compelled to by the appearance of regular customers, all of whom expect personal visits. "If I don't go to take their orders they aren't happy," he tells me.

André goes to the dining room now to take an order. When he returns he calls to Stuart, "Two terrine."

"Oui," Stuart replies.

André then calls out the entrée orders and ends by saying "Two asparagus" to Stuart, who again says, *"Oui."*

It is now seven-thirty, and despite how busy it is, Stuart finds time to say to George, who has walked over to one of Stuart's refrigerators to get some watercress, "Tomorrow night. Eleven o'clock. *In the Heat of the Night.*"

"What?" says George, looking startled.

"In the Heat of the Night," says Stuart. "It's a great movie. You never saw it?"

George shakes his head no.

"Last night there was a great movie too," says Stuart, but George is already back at his station at the other end of the kitchen and shows no sign of having heard.

The worker manning the dishwasher scrapes leftover butter out of a pile of butter dishes and into a silver bucket. This butter will be used for preparing staff meals.

Through the door window, a waiter calls, "Soufflé twenty-four in the oven."

"Okay. Take out twenty-five," says Denis to the waiter. He is helping Stuart, who is bombarded with orders for both appetizers and desserts as the first and second seatings overlap. Denis puts the soufflés in the small oven and passes out a tray of four soufflés destined for table twenty-five.

"Did you hear about twenty-four?" says the waiter.

"Yes. It's in the oven."

These guys are working very quickly and efficiently. It's almost dizzying to look around and see Stuart whipping the desserts for the tables that have run late from the first seating, the dishwasher stacking his machine, the pot scrubber scrubbing, smoke rising from the stove. There is a very strong smell of cooking oil and dishwashing soap and, always, *always,* the heat.

"Soufflé twelve in the oven," calls a waiter.

"Yes, sir," says Stuart, but, engrossed in getting out another dessert order, he forgets.

In the meantime, André pulls a tray out from under one of the broilers, a waiter passes in a tray, George returns from downstairs with more chickens.

"Manuel," Denis calls to the potwasher. Hands still in the sink, Manuel looks over his shoulder. Denis picks up a small oval serving tray, indicating that he needs more of these. Amid all this bedlam André, who is busy preparing an entrée but misses nothing that goes on in the kitchen, yells, "Stuart, did you put soufflé twelve in the oven?"

"No, Chef."

"Put it in." With that, he leaves for the dining room to see how the customers from the first seating enjoyed their meals. Then he stands in the hallway outside the kitchen to say good-bye to those who are leaving and at the same time greet those arriving for the second seating.

At seven fifty-five Henry asks the waiter assigned to the eight o'clock private party, "What's the story with the party?" From their vantage point in the kitchen the cooks can't tell if party members have arrived, since they go directly upstairs.

"They're here but they're having drinks," the waiter replies. "Give me ten minutes."

"All right," Henry says. "We're counting."

"The theory with the party is that we have to hurry them along," Stuart says to me. "Otherwise we're going to be preparing their main course when we're really busy with the rest of dinner."

Denis is indeed counting the minutes. He puts the quail in the oven, so that they will be ready in ten minutes. He then slips the party menu into the overhead slot where the rest of the dinner-orders-in-progress are hanging. This signifies that the party is under way and cooking has begun.

The menu for the party is half a quail ("Juan calls them little bambinos because the way the dough is wrapped around their legs looks like a little diaper," says Stuart), plus baby bass, sorbet, medallions of veal with a vegetable garnish, mixed salad, and Grand Marnier soufflés.

8:00 P.M.

As the second seating officially begins, André returns to the kitchen. One minute later, the customer who expanded his reservation from eight to ten people sticks his hand through the window to shake André's hand. André beams, never letting on that this man caused any trouble. Customers did indeed linger over dessert, but so far two tables have not shown up for their reservations and only two guests have had to wait for a table. "If you look at my wife, she's a little nervous," says André, wiping his hands on a towel. "We are keeping them waiting in the bar, but we can only keep them waiting so long."

André leaves for the dining room to take the order of the table for ten, once again saying, "If I do not do it, they are not happy."

At the same time, Denis takes the party's ten baby quail out of the oven and Stuart helps him cut them in half. Seeing that the quail are ready, George spreads nineteen white plates on two large silver trays and pours a small pool of brown sauce onto the middle of each plate. Henry takes the quail halves and puts one on top of the sauce on each plate.

Two waiters, one of whom is floating through the restaurant helping wherever needed and another who is momentarily free, take one tray each and head upstairs.

They reappear almost immediately and place the trays back on the long window ledge, saying, "They're not ready."

"Not ready?" Henry says, with a look of disbelief.

"He says he didn't tell you to put it on," says one of the waiters. Earlier, when the waiter said, "Give me ten minutes," he meant to give him ten minutes before he'd tell them when to start cooking. Denis thought he meant he wanted to have the food in ten minutes.

"Anybody hungry?" Henry deadpans as the trays of quail are passed back into the kitchen.

André returns with the large table's order and, looking at the quail, says, "What happened?" Answering his own question, he says, "They weren't ready? How could you send them out if they weren't ready?"

"I thought they were ready," says Denis.

"You can't think," says André. "You have to know."

Stuart leans over and whispers to me, "You can never use the word 'think' in a restaurant. My old chef used to say, 'I don't pay you to think. I pay you to work.' "

Working quickly, Henry and Denis remove the quail to a broiler pan and George scrapes the sauce back into its original metal canister. The quail are placed above the broilers so that the rising heat will keep them warm.

Six minutes later, the waiter who had told them "ten minutes" reappears to say the party is now ready to start eating. "What happened?" he says, looking through the window, obviously puzzled as to why he doesn't see the quail anywhere.

"We threw them out," says Henry. The waiter looks shocked, but then realizes Henry is only kidding.

Starting over, George lays out clean white plates on the two trays and pours the sauce onto their centers. This time André pitches in, taking the quail down from their perch above the broiler and putting the quail halves on top of the sauce.

Baby bass is the next course, and Henry asks André how to serve it. "With just a little lemon?"

"No," says André. *"Sauce béarnaise."* Henry, whose personal preference would have been to make this course lighter, looks puzzled but says nothing.

Nineteen stem glasses appear as if by magic on the ledge in the door. "Where did these come from?" I say.

"The mystery elf," says Stuart, putting the glasses into the freezer so that they will be lightly frosted by the time they're needed for the party's sorbet course.

The baby bass remains in the refrigerator across from Henry's stove, where it will stay until the waiter or "mystery elf" comes to say the table is ready for its entrée. In the meantime, orders from the dining room continue to arrive and are being filled at a dizzying pace.

Like all chef/owners, André tends to do more supervising, meeting, greeting, and order-taking than cooking. But because of the fast pace and increased pressure, he's now needed in the kitchen and he goes to work once again at George's stove. As André works, he pivots on his left foot like a figure in Lord & Taylor's Christmas windows. His left foot remains centered on the floor; he steps with his right foot to the stove, then back to the counter.

George kneels to put something in the oven while Henry reaches up for a whisk that, along with assorted ladles, is hanging from the ceiling over the aisle between the stoves and the counters. Henry then checks something in the oven and closes the oven door with his knee. Instead of walking over to two plates in front of Denis's stove, both of which already hold noodles, André does a long sideways stretch to put some meat onto the plates. Denis lifts a stack of clean plates from the counter by the dishwasher and puts them on a shelf to the right of Henry's stove. As I watch all of this movement, I remember a comment Molly O'Neill, food writer for *The New York Times,* and a former chef, once made to me: "A day as a chef is tantamount to eight hours of aerobics classes. It's highly physical labor."

One of the waiters from the dining room brings back a plate and, in a soft voice, says to Denis, through the door's window, "Denis, the noodles are cold."

Expressionless, Denis takes the plate and sticks just the side with the noodles under the broiler. This method of reheating is quicker than sautéing a new batch, which would allow the rest of the food to get cold. He glances at André, who is cooking at George's stove, grimacing over the heat. André is concentrating hard, his lips pursed together, and he seems not to have heard the waiter. I have a feeling he is remaining silent because of my presence in the kitchen, not wanting to embarrass Denis.

At eight-thirty, the party's waiter comes to the long window and says, "One minute for the baby bass." Henry spreads the skillets over the top of the stove and he and Denis start placing the baby bass in them.

While Henry supervises the bass, Denis dishes out noodles into large serving dishes and puts them under the broiler.

André, in the meantime, is carving a steaming hot duck for customers in the dining room. The duck is too hot to hold with his bare hand so he uses his apron to diffuse some of the heat.

After sending out the duck, André assists Henry and Denis, spreading white plates for the baby bass on the counter. Henry ladles out the béarnaise sauce and Stuart puts the baby bass on top of the sauce. André puts the full plates on the window ledge and calls, *"Garçon!"* His expression and his voice are tense. André has said that he and his staff keep a lot of tension inside, and this is the first outward manifestation of it I've seen.

The only waiter in sight is one from the downstairs dining room. "Get me the waiters right away," André barks at him. The waiter hurries upstairs to summon the party's waiters.

André wipes his hand on his towel and looks around the

kitchen for what to do next. All the cooks hold a white towel in their hands as they work. They use the towels to remove hot pans from the stoves and ovens and to wipe stray drops of sauce from the edge of a plate about to go out to a customer; as André just did, they also frequently wipe their hands on these towels.

As they cook intently, every so often a flame flares up when the oil overshoots a pan. The sounds of running water, banging pots, chopping knives, continue. The flattened cardboard boxes under the feet of the washers are drenched and the floor around them is soaking wet.

Receiving his cue from the party's waiter, Stuart serves up sorbet, as a palate refresher between courses. He tops the portions with rum-soaked raisins and sprinkles them with cherry brandy.

A waiter calls in to Stuart to put a soufflé in the oven.

"Oui," says Stuart. He puts it in the oven and then ladles himself a glass of ice water from the bucket of melted ice.

Soon, the party's waiter tells the kitchen to ready the party's entrée. Hearing him, George takes the veal medallions out of the refrigerator and puts them in the oven. Denis, meanwhile, sautés the mixed vegetables that will be served with it.

The same waiter calls in to Stuart: "Scoobidoo? Nineteen mélange." These salads will be served at the same time as the entrée.

André, who is about to go into the dining room to take another order, washes his hands. He has done this each time he's headed for the dining room, and his hands are beginning to look red and raw.

The veal is served to the party at nine-fifteen. After the plates have been taken upstairs, André tells me to walk around the restaurant. "It's at its peak now," he says.

He walks into the dining room with me and points out that the people eating would never know how tense and frantic things are in the kitchen. "I tell them not to yell in the kitchen, to keep things down," André says.

Walking into the dining room is like walking into another world. It is cool here and hushed and serene. The lights are dim. The customers look relaxed and happy and the captains and waiters give off an illusory air of calmness, as if their jobs were effortless.

André travels easily between the kitchen and dining room, not letting any of the pressure he's feeling show to his customers, and almost never to his staff. Although he claims he's gotten angry at his employees, I've never seen him yell at one of them, not even when he had good reason to.

He walks to the bar, where he retrieves two beers, one for himself and one for George. "Until nine P.M. we drink water," he says. "After nine P.M. the Europeans drink a beer. It gives us a lift. You're thirsty and tense and it helps."

Back in the kitchen, I again notice the strong smells of dishwashing liquid and hot oil. Surprisingly, none of the food throws off any discernible delicious smells.

André gets to work carving a chicken. After he's done he puts the carcass on a shelf by the door, where it tops a stack of other chicken bones that will be used tomorrow to make chicken stock.

"Do we have any salmon mousse left?" André asks Stuart. If not, they will need to let the waiters know.

Stuart looks in one of the refrigerators and says, "Yes, Chef."

"How many?" says André, meaning how many portions.

Sizing up the mousse, Stuart says, "Three."

"Soufflé fourteen in the oven," a waiter calls in.

"What table?" Stuart asks the waiter. Despite the onslaught of orders, Stuart seems very calm and unruffled.

"Fourteen."

He puts the soufflés for that table in the oven and then passes a few plates of salad to another waiter.

Dirty plates are beginning to be returned en masse. The busboys stack these dirty dishes in the waist-high window cut into the wall by the dishwasher. Through this same window, they place the silverware in a shallow tub filled with water and dishwashing liquid.

At nine-forty a waiter yells, "Sixteen in oven." *"Oui,"* says Stuart and he puts the soufflés in.

Nonstop, dirty dishes continue to be passed in through the window, with much banging and clanging.

"Soufflé twenty-one, please," a waiter calls, and Stuart puts the order in the oven.

The cooks have repeatedly wiped scraps of food off the counters and onto the floor. George takes advantage of a momentary respite from cooking to *really* wipe down the stainless steel counter at his station, buffing it to a shine.

A waiter tells Stuart to put the soufflés for the troublemaking table of ten in the oven. Two customers did have to wait a few minutes for a table but they had a drink at the bar and didn't complain.

The party of ten had all ordered Grand Marnier soufflés, and André pays special attention to them. He makes Stuart put more batter in each mold. André then writes the ordered inscription celebrating the close of a business deal on top of each soufflé. After putting them in the oven, André ladles himself another glass of ice water. He throws back his head and drinks it all.

The potwasher makes forays through the narrow kitchen to pick up the dirty pans. Again, the pots bang and clang and the water keeps running and running in the sink.

As André waits for another order to arrive, he taps his fingers on the counter. Never, ever, are his hands still.

Everyone is drinking more water now. The sound of a group laughing in the dining room filters in to the kitchen. When you're in here, it's easy to forget that there are people in the dining room relaxing and enjoying themselves. The only sight the kitchen staff has of the customers is when they arrive and depart, as the second seating is beginning to do now.

One man on his way out looks in through the long window across from the stoves and says, "Have any of you ever worked on a ship?"

They all say no. After the man is safely out of sight, Stuart comments, "Where they get these questions I don't know."

Next, a departing female customer wants to know where the bread is from. "Tom Cat Bakery in Queens," says André.

"It's delicious," says the woman, "and my family had a bakery when I was growing up so I should know."

"Hot, hot, hot," cries George, as a warning to everyone to get out of his way as he rushes down the aisle toward the potwasher. Everyone presses themselves against the counter to let him pass.

At nine fifty-five, Henry, who is finished cooking, carries some trays of fish downstairs and comes back with truffles for a dish André is making.

Denis helps Stuart take the soufflés for the upstairs party out of the oven, and the waiters whisk them away. A few minutes later, André joins the party too, to ask how everything is and to receive his much-loved and much-needed praise.

At ten o'clock Henry goes home. "The minute Henry leaves, it means there are no more orders coming in and everyone knows they can start dismantling," says Stuart, who does just that. He unplugs his hot plate, wipes it with a towel, and returns it to the shelf over his counter.

"You going northeast?" he says to Denis. This is Stuart's way of asking if he can have a ride home. "Northeast" means Denis is going to see his girlfriend. "North" means he's going home and can drop off Stuart.

"North," says Denis. "Totally north."

"Good," says Stuart. "Six dollars cab fare on my salary is a lot."

"Why don't you take a bus?" asks the normally silent George.

"I'm in a hurry."

I ask Stuart how he feels now that the pressure has eased. "Sort of like I was run over by a train," he replies.

Having heard only good things from the people at the party, André heads to the downstairs dining room to talk to the customers there and ask them how they enjoyed their meals. "If I went home now they wouldn't like it," he says. "Talking to them now makes them feel like they've been taken care of."

Every table has only accolades: "Wonderful," the customers say. "Delicious." Heading back to the kitchen, André happily says, "They all smile so it's okay." These smiles are the rewards for which he works so hard.

Many customers, however, are rewarding André with something more concrete than smiles—they are stopping at Simone's hostess stand and making reservations for upcoming nights. As they do so, the waiters carry a few wine buckets back to the kitchen. The dishwasher takes a wine bottle with about three inches of wine left in it and slugs it back. Oblivious to the vineyard or the vintage, he downs the whole thing, knowing only that it is cold and refreshing and very, very good.

11:00 P.M.

*S*tuart and Denis head for home, neither one of them knowing that Denis would soon resign to go work at Aureole, and that Stuart would be promoted to take his place.

George remains in the upstairs kitchen, where he will stay until all the desserts have been sent out. The dishwashers, in turn, stay until the last plate and glass have been washed and put away. They will clean the kitchen counters and the floor, leaving it sparkling clean to welcome Jacques when he returns the next morning.

The dining-room staff stay put until all the tables in their stations are empty. They then go home, leaving behind the two waiters whose turn it is to close the restaurant. This involves removing all the tablecloths and stacking the tables and chairs on one side so that, tomorrow morning, Guido can mop the floor.

Having asked the few customers lingering over coffee and dessert if everything was all right, André checks the reservations book to see how many confirmed reservations there are for tomorrow. With that number in mind, he walks down to the prep kitchen to order the meats and fish he will need to feed them.

"I order only when everything is finished so I can see what's left," he says. "It's very important. That's why I don't let anyone else order for me. If we have too much left over we lose money and if we have too little of something we run out."

Pen and paper in hand, he walks into the refrigerator and looks through the drawers holding the fish and then those holding meat. He makes a shopping list:

> 1 (10 lbs.) salmon (fillet)
> 5 lbs. fillet of bass
> 4 lbs. of sea scallops
> 4 lbs. of bay scallops
> 15 baby bass in fillet
> 3 lbs. fillet of whiting
> 1 salmon (6 lbs. fillet)
> 12 lbs. mussels
> 3 lbs. jumbo crab meat
> 16 saddles of rabbit
> 1 fresh foie gras
> 4 pigeons

He counts the racks of lamb but decides that he has enough. Next he writes:

> 2 packs fresh saddle of hare
> 2 loins of veal

After he's done checking the refrigerator he scans a typed master list of everything the restaurant needs to have in stock. Looking at the list, André realizes he forgot to order fillet of sole and adds that (two pounds) to his list.

Now he picks up the phone and starts calling his suppliers. When the first telephone answering machine picks up he says, "Restaurant Lutèce. Two racks of lamb and two loins of veal. That's it. Bye-bye."

His second phone call is picked up by a machine too. He identifies himself: "Restaurant Lutèce," and then lists the fish he wants to order.

A person answers his third call and, with no small talk, André places his order.

After two more calls André is finished with his ordering. It's now eleven-thirty. All the customers are gone, as is George. The waiters are finishing clearing the dining room and the dishwashers are almost done cleaning the kitchen. At her post Simone is finishing up the cashier's paperwork so that Odette will be able to do the breakdown tomorrow morning.

After she is finished, husband and wife head for their home on the fourth floor. There, André will make himself a tuna fish sandwich: "I take a can of whatever tuna fish my wife bought at the supermarket, add a little chopped white onion, a splash of tarragon vinegar, and eat this with country bread." Most bakeries refer to this hearty white bread as peasant bread.

He'll drink another beer with his sandwich and eat a banana for dessert. Then, while his vegetables for tomorrow are being loaded onto a truck at Dom's Market, while his lamb is arriving at the warehouse of a purveyor, who will resell it to DeBragga and Spitler, and as his fish supplier gets his last hour of sleep before waking to another business day, André will lie down next to his wife.

Just before he disappears, André turns around and says, "Forty-three years I work like this. March 1, 1948, I started my apprenticeship. What do you think?"

"I think it's a lot of hard work," I say. "Until I started research for this book I had no idea how hard restaurateurs worked. Now I know enough to open my own restaurant."

"Oh, *ja?*" replies André. "I have one I can sell to you."

EPILOGUE

*T*hursday night, November 14, 1991, is the end of another day similar to the one we just witnessed. The only difference is that André and his staff have recently sighted Bryan Miller, the *New York Times*'s restaurant critic, at the restaurant, and have been called by the paper's fact checker, so they know that Lutèce will most likely be reviewed in tomorrow's paper. And, because of last week's devastating two-and-a-half-star review in *New York Newsday,* all of them know that the restaurant's future, as well as their own continued employment, may very well depend on the number of stars Miller has given them.

As the minutes pass by and André makes his way into and out of the kitchen and dining room, he is doing his best to keep his anxiety at bay. Nonetheless, he is thinking: Will I still have four stars? Will I continue doing what I've done almost all of my life, or might I possibly, truly, sadly, *seriously* think about retiring, about selling the restaurant, about teaching someplace, about having more time to have a life, as Simone would say?

By eleven o'clock captain Roger Benjamin has finished working and hurries out to the newsstand around the corner. Holding his breath, he buys the early edition of the *Times,* opens it immediately, and is the first one to learn what the future holds.

He hurries back to the restaurant and tells Simone. Roger calls the number into the kitchen, and as the news spreads like wildfire among the staff, he looks for André. He finds him in the downstairs dining room, his white toque bobbing as he laughs at something a customer has said, never letting on that his future is about to be decided.

He looks up and sees Roger holding up four fingers. Focused on the dining room, André thinks Roger is telling him to go to table four. André turns, but the table is empty.

Puzzled, André looks back at Roger, who again holds up four fingers. This time André sees that Roger's face is lit up with joy.

And that's when it hits him, like a physical blow. He thinks, Okay. That's it. We did it.

He heads for Simone at the hostess stand, accepting his staff's congratulations along the way. Simone, ever professional, quietly congratulates her husband. Beaming, André looks down at the review. There are the stars . . . one, two, three . . . four!

And the first paragraph of the review, in effect, socks it to *Newsday,* which had called Lutèce old-fashioned, "a food museum." "How does one rate an institution like Lutèce?" Miller writes. "The quality of food and service is foremost to be sure. But there is also another consideration, one that requires an appreciation of history."

"I was very pleased," André says later. "Maybe I never was as pleased. Had we not gotten four stars, it would have raised a lot of questions for me. But it went well and all these questions I didn't have to ask."

Did he celebrate? "No," says André. "We are not people who celebrate. We were happy but we continued to work. We did the same thing the next day. I got up at the same time, I did the same work. I worked as much or maybe even a little more."

Like all top-ranking restaurants, Lutèce is fueled by one person's tremendous enthusiasm and drive for success. André would sum up his secret in one little phrase: "Being there." But the real secret is the devotion he shows and the example he sets by his presence. He devotes his life to details, obsessively pursuing high-quality ingredients and first-rate staff and being willing to pay top dollar for them, and always, *always,* keeping in mind that his function is not just to feed people but to make them happy. André calls the desire to make people happy something else, and he is the living embodiment of how successful a person can be when he pours that something else into a restaurant, much as one would a special sauce. André calls it love.

ABOUT THE AUTHOR

IRENE DARIA works in New York City and lives on Long Island with her husband, Cary Wiener. She is the author of a previous book, *The Fashion Cycle,* and is an award-winning columnist for *Glamour* and a contributor to many other national magazines.

ABOUT THE TYPE

This book was set in Garamond, a typeface originally designed by the Parisian type cutter Claude Garamond (1480–1561). This version of Garamond was modeled on a 1592 specimen sheet from the Egenolff-Berner foundry, which was produced from types assumed to have been brought to Frankfurt by the punch cutter Jacques Sabon (d. 1580).

Claude Garamond's distinguished romans and italics first appeared in *Opera Ciceronis* in 1543–44. The Garamond types are clear, open, and elegant.